# Innovation Nation

# Department for Innovation, Universities & Skills

*Presented to Parliament by the Secretary of State for Innovation, Universities & Skills,
the Chancellor of the Exchequer and the Secretary of State for
Business Enterprise and Regulatory Reform
by Command of Her Majesty*

*March 2008*

Cm 7345

£18.55

# Contents

# The Government wants to create a stronger and fairer Britain, equipped to meet the challenges of the future.

We want to create an Innovation Nation because Britain can only prosper in a globalised economy if we unlock the talents of all of our people.

We want innovation to flourish across every area of the economy and, in particular, wherever high value added businesses can flourish and grow. We must innovate in our public services too. Innovation is as important to the delivery of healthcare and education as it is to industries such as manufacturing, retail and the creative economy.

Innovation will be the key to some of the biggest challenges facing our society, like global warming and sustainable development. We need to ensure that Britain contributes to the innovative solutions and that British business and the British people benefit from the new opportunities and prosperity they create.

In this White Paper, we set out our aim to make Britain the best country in the world to run an innovative business or public service. We can do this by investing in people and knowledge, unlocking talent at all levels, by investing in research and in the exploitation of knowledge and by using regulation, public procurement and public services to shape the market for innovative solutions.

In all this there is an exciting challenge for business, public services, third sector organisations, towns and cities, universities and colleges. Government can foster innovation but only people can create an Innovation Nation.

*John Denham*

**Rt Hon John Denham MP**
Secretary of State for Innovation, Universities and Skills

Innovation is essential to the UK's future economic prosperity and quality of life. To raise productivity, foster competitive businesses, meet the challenges of globalisation and to live within our environmental and demographic limits, the UK must excel at all types of innovation.

This will mean harnessing ideas from the public and private sectors, users and professionals to create more effective products, services, processes and methods of public service delivery. The UK must unlock the talent of all of its people and become an Innovation Nation.

Government cannot and should not accomplish this task alone. The Department of Innovation, Universities and Skills' role is to champion innovation across the board, working with partners across and outside government. Building on the Government's knowledge economy programme, the 2004 Science and Innovation Investment Framework and Lord Sainsbury's recent Review as well as the 2008 Enterprise Strategy, DIUS has sought advice from leading thinkers and practitioners to develop this White Paper to promote innovation across the UK's society and economy.

The UK has a number of strengths: a leading position in scientific research, a number of highly competitive business sectors, a stable and supportive macroeconomic climate and flexible product and labour market regulation. The UK also excels at "hidden innovation" – in its leading services sectors and creative industries.

However, there are a number of areas in which the UK must improve. The UK's productivity performance has been improving steadily since 1997 but still lags some leading international competitors. Moreover, there remain long-standing weaknesses in the skills base and in the number of employers investing in training.

The Government's aim is to make the UK the leading place in the world which to be an innovative business, public service or third sector organisation. We aim to build an Innovation Nation in which innovation thrives at all levels – individuals, communities and regions.

### The Changing Face of Innovation

In the past, innovation was thought of as a simple process of investment in fundamental research leading to commercialisation by far-sighted management in industry. This process has traditionally been supported by supply-side policy initiatives.

However, innovation draws on a wide variety of sources and is driven as much by demand as by supply. The insights generated by basic science are critical to long-term innovation performance but the path they follow from the laboratory to the marketplace is long, complex and uncertain.

Other sources of innovation include the creative application of tried-and-tested technologies and the role of design in developing innovative products and services. Innovation is also not restricted to the private sector – increasingly the public sector is called upon (often in partnership with the private and third sectors) to innovate in the design and delivery of public services.

Enabled and accelerated by new technologies, innovation is becoming more open. Organisations are increasingly reaching outside their walls to find ideas – to universities, other companies, suppliers and even competitors. Users are also increasingly innovating independently or in collaboration with businesses or in the co-creation of public services.

Government policy needs to recognise these new sources of innovation and, in particular, develop new instruments that drive demand for innovation as well as its supply.

## Government Creates the Conditions for Innovation to Flourish

Government creates the conditions for innovation by ensuring macroeconomic stability and open and competitive markets. In many sectors of the economy, maintaining this framework and investing in people and knowledge are sufficient for innovation to flourish. In some specific areas, government can provide more direct support using regulation, public procurement and public services to shape the market for innovative solutions. Innovation is also essential to meeting some of the biggest challenges facing our society, like global warming and sustainable development. Our policies must similarly build the capabilities of British business and the British people to benefit from the new opportunities that will be created.

This White Paper includes new proposals about how Government can use procurement and regulation to promote innovation in business as well what it can do to make the public sector and public services more innovative. Working through institutions like the Technology Strategy Board (TSB), our aim should be to bring everyone together, from designers to manufacturers and from providers to customers and users, to understand and take advantage of these opportunities.

## Demanding Innovation

Demand drives innovation by encouraging innovators to meet new, advanced needs. Early users, whether they be individuals, businesses or Government itself, shape innovations in their most important phase of development and provide critical early revenue. Regulation can help or hinder innovation by setting stretching standards for new technologies or constricting freedom to innovate. If the UK is to become an Innovation Nation, it must complement the supply-side innovation measures with demand-side policies.

To drive increased demand for innovative products and services:

• Each Government Department will include an Innovation Procurement Plan as part of its commercial strategy, setting out how it will drive innovation through procurement and use innovative procurement practices.

• DIUS will reform the Small Business Research Initiative, refocused on technology based research, prototyping this with the Ministry of Defence and the Department of Health and will extend the revised SBRI to all participating Departments by April 2009.

• DIUS and the CBI will facilitate the interchange of innovation expertise between the public and private sector, including the secondment of private sector experts into the public sector for the purpose of mentoring in pro-innovation procurement.

• DIUS and the Better Regulation Executive in the Department of Business, Enterprise and Regulatory Reform (BERR) will work with the Business Council for Britain and others to identify how regulation may promote or hinder innovation.

# Executive Summary

- DIUS and the Better Regulation Executive in BERR will use existing regulators' fora to share experience on how their activities could promote innovation.

- DIUS will publish a Science & Society Strategy in the Autumn, along with an implementation and delivery plan.

## Supporting Business Innovation

Business is an engine of innovation, a generator of wealth and a driver of improved living standards. Government plays a critical role in guaranteeing the framework in which businesses can innovate and in providing direct support where the market fails.

The UK has significant strengths across all sectors of its economy and innovation performance is on an upwards trend. Strategic organisations like the Technology Strategy Board, Regional Development Agencies, Devolved Administrations, UK Intellectual Property Office, Energy Technologies Institute (ETI) and National Endowment for Science, Technology and the Arts (NESTA) play important roles in driving innovation and coordinating government effort.

To make the UK the best place in the world to be an innovative business:

- The Technology Strategy Board will bring forward 5 new Innovation Platforms over the next 3 years, including developing technology demonstrators to show innovative solutions in action.

- Over the English regions, at least 500 businesses will be given an innovation voucher to work with a knowledge base institution of their choice, with the aspiration that this would increase to at least 1000 per year by 2011 as the vouchers were demonstrated to be effective for businesses. This is expected to mean an investment of at least £3 million to initiate collaborations between SMEs and the knowledge base.

- DIUS will work to ensure appropriate finance is available for all innovative businesses at all stages of their growth. This will be set out clearly in a "guide to innovation finance" based on the "No Nonsense Guide" on access to finance.

- DIUS will take forward the Sainsbury Review recommendation to develop a national Proof of Concept specification to be delivered by the RDAs, which will provide access to facilities and have a strong focus on investor readiness.

- DIUS and the Technology Strategy Board working with partners will take forward the Sainsbury recommendation to double the number of Knowledge Transfer Partnerships, increasing their flexibility and applicability to a range of educational institutions including FE colleges.

- DIUS will continue to work with BERR, Technology Strategy Board and NESTA to investigate innovation in service sectors.

- The UK-IPO will examine whether there is a role for Government in helping small firms obtain investment through better reporting of their intangible assets, by the end of 2008.

- By the summer of 2009 all UKTI export and Business Link advisors will receive training from the UK-IPO in advising businesses on IP management. UK-IPO will provide online support to help small business exploit their IP through licensing and other means which are increasingly important to innovative business. This network will be used to promote an awareness-raising programme on the importance and changing nature of intellectual property.

## A Strong and Innovative Research Base

The UK's world-class research base is an important component of its innovation ecosystem. Alongside other sources of knowledge like large companies, SMEs and users, it drives the creation of new ideas, some of which have potential to deliver significant economic and social benefits.

Working with the Research Councils and the Technology Strategy Board, DIUS will build on the UK's current impressive performance on research and broaden the traditional knowledge exchange agenda to encompass new disciplines, new sectors, new businesses and those who work in the development and delivery of public services.

To maintain and improve the UK's standing in research:

- DIUS will maintain the growing investment in UK science and will broaden knowledge exchange between the research base and businesses into the arts and humanities and service sectors such as the creative industries.

- The UK-IPO will continue to develop the 'Lambert' online toolkit of model university-business licensing agreements, which cuts the cost and complexity of IP transactions.

- DIUS has commissioned a study to look at how universities should manage IP for their own benefit and for the benefit of the wider economy.

- NESTA will develop a new Innovation Index to measure the UK's performance as an Innovation Nation, drawing on input and expertise from partners such as the ONS, DIUS, BERR, TSB, Advanced Institute of Management (AIM), the Design Council, CBI and others. A pilot index will be published in 2009 with a fuller system in place by 2010.

- A new Innovation Research Centre will be established by DIUS, NESTA, Economic and Social Research Council (ESRC) and the Technology Strategy Board to ensure a steady supply of high quality innovation research into the UK innovation policy community.

## International Innovation

Innovation is increasingly an international endeavour. Businesses are internationalising their R&D, supply chains and customer bases and adopting "open innovation" models. Like the ideas that they create and use, the people who drive innovation are also increasingly mobile, as is the finance that support innovators.

The Government is committed to making the UK one of the most attractive places in the world for mobile R&D-intensive businesses to invest. Its research base promotes collaboration for excellence irrespective of national borders and our open economy facilitates the internationalisation of high-tech businesses. However, international innovation competition is intensifying, spurred on by increasing investment by emerging economies.

To ensure that the UK is the most attractive location for innovative businesses, individuals, and organisations:

- DIUS will assume responsibility for leading and managing the FCO Science and Innovation Network (SIN). In the future, DIUS and FCO will co-fund this network and DIUS will host a management team of DIUS and FCO staff to oversee the network's operation.

- During 2008, DIUS will produce an international strategy, which will draw together inter-related policies within DIUS' remit, encompassing higher and further education, skills, research and innovation.

- The Technology Strategy Board will develop, as part of its international strategy, a marketing plan to help deliver a step change in the ability of UK business to compete for grants in EU Framework Programme 7.

- DIUS will work with BERR on implementing the European Commission's lead market initiative so that the UK's most innovative businesses can take advantage of the European single market and of new technology-driven global markets.

- The Technology Strategy Board will advise Government on the opportunities which may arise from the adoption of EU regulations to stimulate business innovation including, where appropriate, building these into the design of Technology Strategy Board programmes.

### Innovative People

Most new ideas do not come as a flash of inspiration to a lone genius inventor; they come from how people create, combine and share their ideas. The UK's capacity to unlock and harness the talent, energy and imagination of all individuals is crucial to making innovation stronger and more sustainable.

The effects of innovative people are self-reinforcing: innovative businesses are attracted to highly skilled and creative workforces and, in turn, innovative people are drawn towards exciting and challenging career opportunities. Furthermore, innovative people generate new ideas that require skilled people to implement and exploit them.

To maximise the innovative capacity of the UK's people:

- DIUS will drive implementation of the Leitch Review of Skills to raise the nation's skill levels and enhance opportunities for innovation, building implementation of the Sainsbury review recommendations into its wider strategies for FE reform.

- DIUS will pilot a revenue based FE Specialisation and Innovation Fund to build the capacity of the FE sector to support businesses to raise their innovation potential. Through a small number of targeted pathfinder projects, DIUS will seek to unlock the talent of the FE workforce to drive business innovation through partnership and knowledge exchange.

- Resources permitting, DIUS will establish at least one National Skills Academy (NSA) in every major sector of the economy, and is actively encouraging bids from innovative industries, space and the environment. Government is interested in seeing plans for a National Enterprise Academy and a NSA for the Environment develop. Government is working with Peter Jones to develop plans for a National Enterprise Academy and with James Dyson to launch the Dyson School for Design Innovation.

- DIUS will shortly publish a Higher Level Skills Strategy. This will provide the overall framework for driving up the higher level skills that contribute to innovation in business.

- Government will continue to grow the Train to Gain programme and the Apprenticeship programme.

- Reformed Sector Skills Councils will look to identify skills gaps which inhibit innovation.

- The new UK Commission for Employment and Skills will pursue work on High Performance Working practices to increase value added in business.

- The Government will develop a framework for the further expansion and development of Higher Education and has asked the Higher Education Funding Council for England (HEFCE) to consult on how the 20 new HE centres can unlock human potential and drive regeneration.

- DIUS will work with BERR and the National Council of Graduate Entrepreneurship to develop regionally-based University Enterprise Networks.

- DIUS will work with the Department for Children, Schools and Families (DCSF) to promote greater take-up of STEM subjects at school, college and university

- DIUS will lead a cross- Government project on labour market needs for STEM skills and adjust policies in the light of its findings.

## Innovation in Public Services

Innovation in public services will be essential to the UK's ability to meet the economic and social challenges of the 21st century. Education, law, health and transport provide the underpinnings for all innovative activity. They must be delivered efficiently and imaginatively to take account of increased and more complex demands from public service users.

The Government is uniquely placed to drive innovation in public services, through allocating resources and structuring incentives. Major forces such as attitudes to risk, budgeting, audit, performance measurement and recruitment must be aligned to support innovation. Together, and with effective leadership, these will progressively overcome existing cultural and incentive barriers. Those responsible for public service delivery must also learn the lessons of open innovation and adopt innovative solutions from the private and third sectors.

To ensure that the UK's public services are the most innovative in the world:

- In order to assist policy makers in understanding the acceptable levels of risk in pursuing innovative policies, the NAO will conduct a study that will explore the role of risk in stimulating or stifling innovation in the public sector.

- The Sunningdale Institute will work with partners to create a Whitehall Innovation Hub, a new partnership of organisations to capture and disseminate learning about public sector innovation.

- NESTA will establish a Public Services Innovation Laboratory. Working as appropriate with partners such as the Young Foundation, The Innovation Unit, IDeA, Design Council and Innovation Exchange, the Laboratory will trial new methods for uncovering, stimulating, incubating and evaluating the most radical and compelling innovations in public services.

- DIUS will convene a Network of Whitehall Innovators to demonstrate commitment at a senior level of Government.

- The Design Council will develop and trial an innovation-enabling programme of designing demand for practitioners in the public sector, along the lines of the existing private sector model.

- DIUS will consider, with the Cabinet office, the value of an extended "power to innovate", enabling front line staff to explore new ways of delivering high quality services.

## Innovative Places

Despite the spread of global communications, innovation still tends to cluster in particular locations, whether they be urban, rural, regional or national. Not all knowledge can be codified, and innovators are helped by interaction that thrives on trust and proximity. Aside from helping the supply of knowledge, clusters mean that innovative organisations can be close to their market and thereby able to anticipate future demands.

## Executive Summary

In the UK, innovation performance varies considerably from place to place. It reflects sectoral specialisation and history. Traditionally, the UK's innovation policy has been concentrated on high-tech manufacturing and this will remain vitally important. However, in the future, spatial innovation strategies must build on each region's distinctiveness. Moreover, because of the internationalisation of knowledge production, many UK regions will increasingly depend not on the creation of knowledge but on its absorption from elsewhere.

To recognise the spatial properties of innovation and to ensure that the benefits of innovation reach all areas of the UK:

- DIUS will sponsor New Partnerships for Innovation that will bring together venture capital, universities, business and regional government to align efforts and develop innovative solutions to local and regional challenges. DIUS will publish a prospectus for New Partnerships in Autumn 2008

- The Technology Strategy Board and RDAs will work to align their strategies and funding for technological research, demonstrators and Innovation Platforms and achieve the £180m aligned funding commitment.

- As part of its work to develop an Innovation Index, NESTA will work with RDAs and DAs and the Innovation Research Centre to explore the scope for regional or sub-national innovation measures that capture spatial innovation patterns.

- DIUS and BERR will build on the success of the National Council for Graduate Entrepreneurship by establishing a regional network which DIUS will co-fund.

- DIUS will work with RDAs, the Technology Strategy Board, the Devolved Administrations, local authorities and other partners including business and universities to align national and regional innovation programmes and, where appropriate, to use multi-area agreements to promote innovation across the administrative boundaries of local authorities.

### Next Steps and Tracking Progress

This White Paper sets out an ambitious aim for the UK's innovation policy, of building an Innovation Nation in which innovation thrives at all levels. Implementing this will be challenging and require DIUS to build new partnerships with stakeholders in the public sector, business, HE, FE and the third sector.

To monitor progress:

- DIUS will lead the production of a cross-Government Annual Innovation Report in Autumn 2008, to review progress across all aspects of government activity relevant to innovation.

- NESTA will develop a new Innovation Index to measure the UK's performance as an Innovation Nation, drawing on input and expertise from partners such as the ONS, DIUS, BERR, TSB, AIM, the Design Council, CBI and others. A pilot index will be published in 2009 with a fuller system in place by 2010.

- A new Innovation Research Centre will be established by DIUS, NESTA, ESRC and the Technology Strategy Board to ensure a steady supply of high quality innovation research into the UK innovation policy community.

# 1. Introduction

1.1 Innovation is essential to the UK's future economic prosperity and quality of life. To raise productivity, meet the challenges of globalisation and to live within our environmental and demographic limits, the UK must excel at all types of innovation. Government creates the conditions for innovation by ensuring macroeconomic stability and open and competitive markets. In many sectors of the economy, maintaining this framework and investing in people and knowledge are sufficient for innovation to flourish. In some specific areas, government can provide more direct support using regulation, public procurement and public services to shape the market for innovative solutions. Our policies must build the capabilities of British business and the British people to benefit from the new opportunities that will be created.

1.2 This strategy sets out what Government and its partners will do to make the UK an Innovation Nation.

## Our Ambition

1.3 The Government's aim is to make the UK the leading place in the world to be an innovative business, third sector organisation, or public service. We aim to build an Innovation Nation in which innovation thrives at all levels – individuals, communities, cities and regions – recognising the distinctiveness of the four UK nations' governance and responsibilities[1].

1.4 Government cannot and should not accomplish this task alone. The Department for Innovation, Universities and Skills' role is to champion innovation across the board, working with partners across and outside Government. However, it is people right across our economy and society who will make the future innovations that matter to our lives.

1.5 This strategy and the accompanying evidence document[2] builds on the Government's knowledge economy programme, launched in 1998[3] , the 2003[4] Innovation Report, the 2004 Science and Innovation Investment Framework,[5] Lord

Sainsbury's recent review of science and innovation policy[6] and the 2008 BERR Enterprise Strategy, to set out a modern framework for improving Britain's capacity for innovation across society. Progress and plans for implementation of Lord Sainsbury's recommendations are described in an accompanying publication[7].

1.6 Since it was established, DIUS has sought advice from leading thinkers and practitioners in the UK and internationally to understand why innovation matters, where it comes from and how to promote it[8]. This advice has informed the analysis, actions and commitments in this strategy.

## The Changing Face of Innovation

1.7 Government has consistently used one definition of innovation: "the successful exploitation of new ideas". This recognises the importance of the creative spark, new knowledge and new ways of thinking. "New" in this context can be new to the sector or the organisation, taking an idea from another context and adapting it to another.

1.8 Improvements in products, services and quality often come from innovations in business processes, models, marketing and enabling technologies. Innovation happens in all service and manufacturing sectors and in the public and third sectors. Open and competitive markets are a prerequisite for successful innovation.

1.9 The definition of "success'" is important: innovation is a risky and unpredictable process which frequently yields unintended consequences – both good and bad. More innovation is not necessarily better: excessive innovation can be wasteful. Furthermore,

## Innovation

Innovation is essential to the UK's future economic prosperity and quality of life. It can be defined as the successful exploitation of new ideas, which can mean new to a company, organisation industry or sector. It applies to products, services, business processes and models, marketing and enabling technologies.

Science and technology are a vital source of innovation. Innovation happens across the private, public and third sectors. Businesses are increasingly engaging in "open innovation", reaching outside their walls for ideas. Users are innovating independently and in partnership with organisations, creating the demand for new products and services.

Government procurement can drive innovation through creating "lead markets" for innovative products and services. Regulation can drive or get in the way of innovation depending on conditions. And increasingly, innovation is global as the spread of new technologies and knowledge drives market integration and collaboration as well as competition across borders.

This changing face of innovation is challenging businesses, Government and wider society to think and act differently if we are to have a successful economy and society over the next decades. Harnessing all the different types of innovation across all sectors is essential if we wish to create the conditions in which our economy can prosper.

innovations should be for a purpose. This may be profit but it could also be to improve healthcare, tackle environmental problems or improve community cohesion.

## Science and technology are a vital source of innovation

1.10 The insights generated by fundamental scientific research are important in long-term innovation performance. They produce generic technologies that create new industries, from the physics behind the computer chip to genetic treatments for disease. Many of the UK's most successful businesses build directly on scientific discovery.

1.11 However, the path from the laboratory to the marketplace is long, complex and uncertain. Innovations take time to diffuse through the economy and society to create value. For instance, there was an almost 150 year lag between Kelvin's discovery of anisotropic magnetoresistance in 1857, the discovery of giant magneto-resistance in 1988 (for which Albert Fert and Peter Gruenberg were awarded the 2007 Nobel Prize in physics) and their commercial use in miniaturised hard disks for computers and music players like the iPod.

1.12 That is why it is so important to continue to invest in science and accelerate the flow of research into society and to challenge scientists to work more creatively and entrepreneurially with one another and with business. The Science and Innovation Investment Framework sets out Government's long term policy for investment in science and research and approaches to maximise their economic and social benefits.

## "Hidden innovation" is increasingly important to the UK's economy and society

1.13 Innovation frequently occurs outside the "traditional" high-technology and manufacturing sectors[9]. Knowledge intensive services such as finance, business services and engineering have formed an increasingly important and successful element of our economy. In 2007, the UK exported around £75 billion of knowledge services, an increase of 170% on the decade before, and now makes up about a quarter of all UK exports. Exports have outpaced imports such that the surplus on trade has trebled from 1.8% of GDP in 1995 to 3.3% in 2005.

1.14 As highlighted in the recent Creative Industries Strategy[10], the arts and creative industries make a very significant contribution to the UK's economy and cultural life and may also have a role in stimulating innovation elsewhere in the economy. For example, design is often fundamental to the creation of innovative products and services[11]; firms with higher design intensity have a greater probability of carrying out product innovation and design expenditure has a positive association with firm productivity growth[12].

1.15 Design is only one example of the role played by the creative industries in innovation[13]. Analysis of the Community Innovation Survey 2004 and input-output data shows firms that spend twice the average amount on creative inputs are 25% more likely to introduce product innovations, while firms that have supply chain linkages with creative industries typically offer more diverse and higher quality products[14]. Possibilities for knowledge transfer may be particularly strong because 54% of those in "creative industry" roles work in businesses outside the creative industries[15].

1.16 Traditional indicators that measure expenditure on research and development and count production of patents fail to capture these types of "hidden innovation" and therefore may be under-representing the strength of the UK[16]. Increasing the performance of the UK's service sectors would have a major impact in closing the productivity gap between the UK and other leading nations.

### Innovation happens in the private, public and third sectors

1.17 Innovation is not confined to the private sector. The UK has a long history of public and social innovation from libraries and fire services to NHS Direct and the Open University, to Oxfam and Live Aid. But it remains the case that for too many public sector organisations, innovation is sometimes regarded as a marginal activity at odds with the main job of delivery. Innovation is an activity which most actors feel they haven't got the time, resources or responsibility to engage with.

### New technologies are enabling and accelerating new forms of innovation

1.18 The growth in commercial use of the internet has created opportunities to support innovation. Advances in communication technologies have made it increasingly cost-effective for organisations to search and collaborate more widely and in places they had not envisaged before. Information technologies, meanwhile, have enabled the accumulation and analysis of large pools of data which has become a powerful driver of knowledge creation and innovation.

1.19 "Innovation technologies" that allow modelling and rapid prototyping reduce the cost, time and risk involved in design and development in comparison to traditional processes[17]. For example, the use of 3D Product Lifecycle Management software in the automotive sector has halved development time[18].

### Organisations are looking outside their walls for sources and markets for innovation

1.20 In light of these opportunities, innovative businesses are increasingly engaging in "open innovation" – reaching outside their walls to find ideas at different stages of development and then developing them in-house. They might reach across sectoral boundaries, up and down the supply chain to lead users or suppliers or out to SMEs or universities. These innovations might be applied to a company's existing market, a new one or spun-out to form an entirely new enterprise[19].

1.21 Compared to more linear and internal models of innovation, open innovation offers considerable benefits to the innovating organisation and to the wider economy and society. Previously, ideas that did not apply to the firm's core business model but could be of use to someone were lost along the way. In some firms, the volume of unexploited patents has been found to be as high as 75-90%[19].

1.22 These new approaches can generate considerable economic returns: Toyota's networked approach to innovation has resulted in suppliers having 14% higher output per worker, 25% lower inventories and 50% fewer defects compared with competitors[20]. Procter & Gamble's "Connect and Develop" strategy now produces 35% of the company's innovations and billions of dollars in revenue. Significantly, since 2000, its own spend on formal R&D as a percentage of sales has declined from 5-6% to 3-4%[21].

### Users are innovating independently and in partnership with organisations

1.23 Historically, users have been responsible for many important innovations including the first heart-lung machine and the World Wide Web. In a range of different sectors, users have been the source of the most commercially-significant and novel products and processes: oil refining (43%), chemical production (70%), sports equipment (58%), and scientific instruments (77%) were highlighted by one recent study[22]. However, largely due to the widespread use of ICT and toolkits users are becoming increasingly important innovators in many different industries[23].

1.24 In many industries, users tend to develop more qualitatively new goods and services than traditional manufacturers, who excel in making incremental improvements to existing products[24]. One explanation is that user-innovators have the freedom to contemplate wholly new solutions; many users care much more about finding a solution to their needs than how it is attained[25]. In contrast, manufacturer-innovators tend to constrain their new product searches to innovations that will be compatible with their expensive prior investments in solution technology and production processes.

## Innovation is Going Global

1.25 The spread of new technologies has driven market integration that, in turn, encourages and speeds up the pace of innovation as sectors – increasingly service-based – are exposed to international competition.

1.26 This is evident in the internationalisation of many innovation-related activities: in 2003, the world's largest companies spent $70.6 billion in R&D outside their home countries, up from $33.9 billion in 1995[26]. Similarly, around 2.5 million students were studying outside their home country in 2004, up from 1.75 million in 1999[27]. Researchers in the UK tend to be more international in their outlook than researchers in other countries. More than 40% of UK science over the past five years involved international collaboration.

1.27 This flow of ideas brings special advantages to places that have strong capacity to absorb ideas and talent from elsewhere and recombine them to create new knowledge and opportunities. High "absorptive capacities" help places channel global flows into their local economies and become even more connected to the global economy in return[28].

1.28 Though this means that while many OECD countries remain innovation leaders, new innovation hotspots are emerging in places that traditionally lagged behind, such as Sao Paolo in Brazil, Shanghai in China and Bangalore in India. Other less known places such as second tier cities in emerging countries – for example, Recife in Brazil, Chongqing in China, Pune and Ahmedabad in India – are also becoming more prominent[29].

## Demand Drives Innovation

1.29 Innovations are the product of the creative interaction of supply and demand[30] though to date, innovation policy around the world has largely concentrated on supply-side measures.

1.30 Demanding and adventurous consumers drive innovation by providing firms with incentives to enter new markets and creating pressures on firms to improve their products and services. This role is understood by business: responding to the EU 2005 Survey of R&D Trends they indicated that market demand for new products and services was by far the most important factor affecting the level of R&D investment, while market access was the most important factor affecting mobile R&D location decisions.

1.31 Demand-led policies have a sound rationale. Many innovations do not appear "off the shelf", but are crude and inefficient and require considerable adaptation. Insofar as the costs of switching to a new technology are borne at adoption and often irrecoverable, there may be advantages in waiting and learning from the experience of others. Delay may be particularly common with network goods such as communication devices whose value rises with the number of users[31, 32]. Consumers of those products will be reluctant to change their behaviour unless they are convinced others will also change[33].

## Demand-oriented Measures Driving Innovation

1.32 Policymakers have an increasing number of demand-side measures at their disposal. These include public procurement, regulation and standardisation, information disclosure and awareness-building and support for private demand[34].

1.33 Given that the UK Government spends around £150 billion per annum on procurement including around £50 billion by Local Authorities, public procurement could be a powerful instrument for creating demand for innovation.

1.34 Regulation and standards can enable the pull through and diffusion of advanced products, services and processes. It is estimated that around 13 % of UK productivity growth between 1948 and 2002 is attributable to the catalogue of standards developed and maintained by the British Standards Institute[35]. Government can play a similar role through regulation and in encouraging industry to converge on common standards.

1.35 However, the relationship between demand-side measures and innovation is complex. Without sufficient information, policy runs the ever-present risk of picking losers; standards, if introduced too early or designed too prescriptively, can lock an industry into a given technology and truncate the search for potentially new, more competitive alternatives. Finally, excessive focus on lead users carries the danger that their voice will dominate and it is by no means certain that their specific requirements will be well-connected to the needs of users in the mass market[36].

## The DIUS Innovation Family

1.36 DIUS works with a range of other organisations that promote UK innovation (in some cases with a formal sponsorship role). These include Regional Development Agencies, The Technology Strategy Board, UK Intellectual Property Office (UK-IPO), National Endowment of Science Technology and the Arts (NESTA), The Design Council, National Weights and Measures Laboratory and BSI British Standards. All will need to engage with the changing face of innovation described here and work together to align their innovation policies.

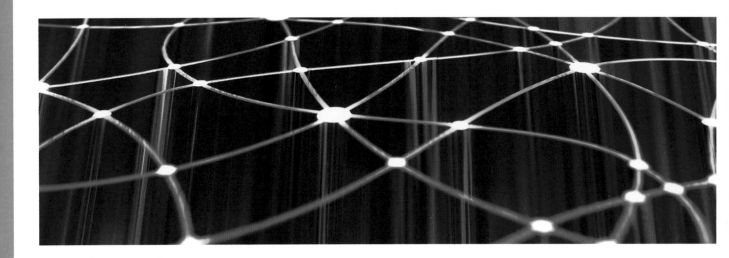

# 2. The Role of Government

2.1 Much innovation will happen without Government involvement. We have many world-leading innovation businesses, large numbers of bright, creative people, strong colleges and universities and a vibrant third sector. If Government policies support education, skills and research, and deliver a stable macro-economic environment and open, competitive markets, innovation will happen. However, there are important areas where Government needs to do more to promote and support the development of an Innovation Nation. The following chapters describe the ways in which Government and its partners can do this.

## A Systemic Approach to Innovation

2.2 The creation of DIUS as a champion for innovation across the board is an important step towards building an Innovation Nation.

2.3 DIUS brings together three of the main drivers of economic success in the 21st Century – support for the skills that people bring to the workforce, science and research and a responsibility for driving innovation. Its work – on further and higher education, science and technology, intellectual property and supporting evidence-based policy making across Government – is central to national prosperity.

2.4 It is just as important to our national wellbeing. Skills offer us all the means to better wages and more secure lives. Learning raises aspirations and helps to create a society where no-one is left behind. With responsibility for all post-19 learning – from basic literacy to postdoctoral level – DIUS will help improve the nation's skills at every level, with provision for people at every stage of their adult lives.

## The Rationale for Government Action

2.5 Markets are powerful drivers of innovation: their openness to economic experiment allow for productive change and gains in productivity[37]. However, markets often do not function perfectly, particularly when considering the generation of ideas and the high degree of uncertainty and coordination that typifies the innovation process[38].

2.6 Government has a lead role in influencing or supporting the environment for innovation:

• Innovation requires a strong research base. The knowledge produced by research in universities and institutes is a key public good: even with intellectual property protection, businesses tend not to capture the full economic benefits of investments in research and will therefore under-invest. It is Government's responsibility to provide it for the economy and society to use.

- In many cases, only Government can influence internationally to promote open and competitive markets and for cooperation and collaboration on investment in research and innovation.

- It is also Government's role to provide the means for people to gain the skills and knowledge for innovation through the entire education system to unlock the talent of all our people.

- Government is responsible for the delivery of public services such as healthcare – in these areas, Government must lead innovation.

- Government is well placed to lead alignment of the innovation system and it sponsors several of the relevant agencies. It will sometimes have to make choices between different societal priorities – between, for instance, the interests of intellectual property rights holders and the interests of follow-on innovators. It is well placed to bridge gaps and facilitate connections between, for example, universities, manufacturers, users and regulators.

- Government can help overcome barriers to business innovation in a variety of ways – by providing funding to encourage collaboration and the timely development and commercialisation of environmental innovations[39], or reduce the risks of investment, by providing systems for advice and guidance to businesses and by supporting networks.

- Consumers may be reluctant to adopt a new technology that has unproven quality or reliability. Government can send a clear signal to consumers about a technology's future (eg by assisting standard-setting organisations or becoming an early adopter); Government can also compel firms to act and launch or adopt changes in technology.

- Most debate about innovation focuses on how we organise innovation; a democratic, well-informed society also needs to ask why we innovate and provide a way of assessing the risks of new technologies, such as nanotechnology, upstream of their introduction. Government has a role in framing and enabling these debates.

- Finally, innovation involves constant upheaval as new technologies and business models drive out old. Government, on grounds of equity and long-term efficiency, has a responsibility to encourage those who lose out to make the transition to new jobs and industries rather than resist change and this frequently has a regional dimension

## The UK's Innovation Performance

2.7 The UK is strong at many aspects of innovation. Based on a decade of increasing investment, it occupies a leading position in scientific research. It is second only behind the US in its production of papers rated as being of the highest scientific quality and is top in per capita terms. Its research base is highly connected with researchers in other countries and measures that aim to track university connections with business are on an upwards trend The number of university to business licensing agreements has risen 271% from 2001 to 2006.

2.8 On the basis of measures of international trade performance and productivity, the UK has a number of highly competitive business sectors. These include high value-added R&D-intensive industries (pharmaceuticals, aerospace) and a number of knowledge-intensive service sectors (financial and business services). Creative industries are very successful in the UK and appear to account for a relatively high proportion of UK output and employment[40].

2.9 Britain is the world's 6th largest manufacturer. Manufacturing adds over £150 billion a year to the UK economy, accounting for around a seventh of total UK output and three-quarters of all business R&D. It generates over 50% of UK exports and directly employs almost three million people.

2.10 Important parts of the UK's innovation system are well aligned to support innovation. Over the past decade the macroeconomic climate has been less volatile than in most other G7 economies. OECD comparisons suggest that product and labour market regulation in the UK imposes lower costs on business than in nearly all other advanced economies.

2.11 The 2007 UK Innovation Survey reports that 64% of UK businesses were active in innovation, up by 45% from 2000[41]. According to the 2007 European Innovation Scoreboard, the UK is one of the "innovation leaders" in Europe with Sweden, Finland, Denmark, and Germany; all these score higher than the US

2.12 Recent Eurobarometer surveys suggest an overall level of public readiness for innovation above the EU average[42]. About 69% of UK consumers say that they are attracted to innovative products, compared to 57% in the EU as a whole. About 16% of UK consumers describe themselves as enthusiasts for innovation, compared with 11% across the EU7.

2.13 But there are areas where the UK needs to improve. The UK's productivity performance has been improving steadily since 1997. However, it still lags some leading international competitors. Service sectors in particular display widely differing productivity rates. The UK exhibits low levels of R&D and patenting, although this may be partly due to industrial structure.

2.14 Up to one fifth of the productivity gap is due to lack of skills. In his 2006 review of skills, Lord Leitch concluded that despite real progress, we need to "raise our game" and become a world leader in skills by 2020 if we are to compete as a 21st Century economy[43]. The review identified long-standing weaknesses in the UK's skills base and the improvement needed if the UK is to compete successfully on skills and innovation. And although participation in Higher Education has increased rapidly, too many people of working age have few qualifications and a third of businesses do not invest at all in training.

2.15 Britain can only succeed in a rapidly changing world if we develop the skills of our people to the fullest possible extent, carry out world class scientific research and apply both knowledge and skills to create an innovative and competitive economy. But it will never be enough to pursue each of these areas in isolation. To an ever increasing extent, our success and future prosperity will depend on creating and aligning complementary policies in these areas.

### Making the UK an Innovation Nation

2.16 This strategy addresses the Government's role and activities in the following areas:

- **Creating demand as an early adopter**
  – Government has a role in creating markets where they may not exist or demonstrating the viability of innovations that others will not necessarily adopt. Through procurement

it has the potential to act as a leader on its own, pulling innovative products and services through from the UK economy in areas such as defence, health or the environment (where the 2007 CEMEP report proposed more widespread use of Forward Commitment Procurement to lead markets [44]). Government regulation can also be a major driver, or inhibitor, of innovation, changing behaviours and giving strong signals to existing or potential markets; it can also drive innovation by raising standards.

- **Setting the frameworks for business innovation** Business is an engine of innovation, a generator of wealth and a driver of improved living standards. Government plays a critical role in guaranteeing the framework in which businesses can innovate and in providing direct support where the market fails. The UK has significant strengths across all sectors of its economy and innovation performance is on an upwards trend. Strategic organisations like the Technology Strategy Board, RDAs, UK-IPO, Energy Technologies Institute and NESTA as well as those in Scotland, Wales and Northern Ireland play important roles in driving innovation and coordinating government effort. In the future, DIUS will continue to improve the environment for innovative businesses.

- **Driving high quality research** A world-class research base is an important component of the UK's innovation infrastructure. Alongside other sources of knowledge like large companies, SMEs and users, it drives the creation of new ideas some of which have potential to deliver significant economic and social benefits. Working with the Research Councils and the Technology Strategy Board, DIUS will build on the UK's current impressive performance on research to maximise its contribution to innovation. Importantly, this

strategy will seek to broaden the traditional knowledge exchange agenda to encompass new disciplines, new sectors, new businesses and those who work in the development and delivery of public services.

- **Marketing the UK internationally** Innovation is increasingly an international endeavour. The UK is at the forefront of the new global knowledge economy. Its research base promotes collaboration for excellence irrespective of national borders and our open economy facilitates the internationalisation of high-tech businesses. However, international innovation competition is intensifying, spurred on by increasing investment by emerging economies. DIUS will build on the UK's strengths in scientific and technological research collaboration to ensure that the UK is well-positioned to maximise its benefit from internationalised innovation.

- **Developing skills** The UK's capacity to unlock and harness the energy, talent and imagination of all individuals is crucial to making innovation stronger and more sustainable. Government influences the UK's supply of innovative people through its funding of higher education, further education, Sector Skills Councils and National Skills Academies. To complement the previous focus on higher education, DIUS will establish a Further Education Specialisation and Innovation Fund. Government is working with Sir James Dyson to launch the Dyson School for Design Innovation. Over the coming months, DIUS will develop a Higher Level Skills Strategy, building on the demand-led model of skills provision outlined by Lord Leitch.

- **Providing high-quality public services** Innovation in public services will be essential to the UK's ability to meet the economic and social challenges of the 21st century.

Education, law, health and transport provide the underpinnings for all innovative activity. They must be delivered efficiently and imaginatively to take account of increased and more complex demands from public service users. The Government is uniquely placed to drive innovation in public services, through allocating resources and structuring incentives. Major forces such as attitudes to risk, budgeting, audit, performance measurement and recruitment must be aligned to support innovation. Together, and with effective leadership, these will progressively overcome existing cultural and incentive barriers. The NAO will conduct an audit-oriented study on innovation in the public sector. NESTA will establish a Public Services Innovation Laboratory to develop and trial the most radical and compelling innovations in public services. DIUS will establish a Whitehall Innovation Hub to disseminate learning from this and other sources to improve understanding of innovation at the highest levels of Government. DIUS will also convene a network of senior Whitehall innovators.

- **Promoting innovative places** In the UK, innovation performance varies considerably from place to place. This is somewhat dependent on sectoral specialisation and history. Traditionally, the UK's innovation policy has been concentrated on high-tech manufacturing. In the future, spatial innovation strategies must build on each region's distinctiveness. Moreover, because of the internationalisation of knowledge production, many UK regions will increasingly depend less on the creation of knowledge than on its absorption from elsewhere. DIUS will work with RDAs and the Technology Strategy Board to build a balance between coordination and intelligent competition across the UK. New Partnerships for Innovation will drive innovation by bringing together public, private and third sector organisations to come up with innovative solutions to local or regional challenges.

## Next Steps

2.17 This strategy sets out an ambitious agenda for the UK's innovation policy. However, policy alone will only go so far and it will be important to monitor the implementation of the commitments made in this strategy. Stakeholder consultation and impact assessment will be undertaken as individual proposals are taken forward.

2.18 In order to do this, DIUS is committed to taking forward the Sainsbury Review recommendation to publish an Annual Innovation Report; the first of these will be published in Autumn 2008.

2.19 The Annual Innovation Report will provide a comprehensive annual assessment of how DIUS is playing its leadership role and how effectively it is delivering its Departmental objectives and strengthening the UK's innovation capability across the public, private and third sectors. The Report (which will include an independent element) will assess the progress made on innovation policy and on science and research and the contribution of the research base to the economy and quality of life in the UK. It will report on projects that have received funding, and the effectiveness with which Government Departments have promoted innovation in the UK, the EU and internationally[45].

2.20 It will also report on the policy initiatives contained in this strategy, as well as the innovation performance of DIUS-sponsored public bodies and delivery partners, including the Technology Strategy Board, the Research Councils, RDAs, UK-IPO, the National Measurement System, NESTA and the Design Council.

# 3. Demanding Innovation

## Demand Drives Innovation

3.1 Demand drives innovation by encouraging innovators to meet new, advanced needs. Early users, whether they be individuals, businesses or Government itself, shape innovations in their most important phase of development and provide critical early revenue. Regulation can help or hinder innovation by setting stretching standards for new technologies or constricting freedom to innovate. If the UK is to become an Innovation Nation, it must complement the supply-side innovation measures with demand-side policies.

## Where the UK Stands

3.2 There are many good examples of innovative procurement. Departments such as the DoH/ NHS and MoD have adopted explicit and strategic approaches to procurement. However, this culture has not yet taken root more generally and procuring innovative solutions has tended to be a low priority. This has been compounded by a risk averse culture, difficulties in defining what constitutes innovation in procurement terms and insufficient capability in procurement skills, especially beyond Whitehall.

3.3 The Small Business Research Initiative (SBRI) was launched in April 2001 as a cross-Departmental programme and is primarily intended to stimulate and increase the demand for R&D from high-technology SMEs and give them the opportunity to demonstrate that they have the ability to undertake and deliver high quality R&D to the public sector. SBRI was made mandatory in Budget 2005 for participating Government Departments. In 2006/07, £2.3 billion was committed to SBRI and the value of contracts made with SMEs was £136.9 million. However, the scheme has not managed to reproduce the kind of success attributed to the Small Business Innovation Research (SBIR) programme in the United States. Specifically, there remains concern that the introduction of targets have not hard-wired innovative procurement practices into routine Departmental behaviour and that tenders for research remain focussed on policy development rather than the strengthening of research in scientific and technical areas.

3.4 The UK enjoys one of the best regulatory environments in the world. The World Bank ranks the UK 6th overall out of 178 economies in terms of ease of doing business. The UK is ranked second amongst G7 members and second among European Member States. The gains from improving regulation, in particular, streamlining administrative burdens, are significant. It is estimated that a 25% reduction in there burdens would result in a 0.9% increase in UK GDP by 2025.

3.5 Government should be particularly careful about the impact of regulation on smaller businesses which are often responsible for the most disruptive innovations[46]. There have been efforts to lighten the regulatory burden on firms, for instance the principles laid out by the Hampton Review. The new Companies Act 2006 alone will save businesses around £250 million a year, including up to £100 million a year for small businesses.

3.6 Innovation Platforms have strengthened levels of cooperation between public and private actors, improving knowledge about long term preferences and demand patterns.

3.7 Recent Eurobarometer surveys suggest an overall level of public readiness for innovation above the EU average. However, this does not appear to be matched by similar levels of scientific knowledge.

3.8 The UK consumer protection regime is effective at supporting and raising confidence in new technologies. In some cases consumers can find information about new products difficult to understand, however.

3.9 The UK has a long history of user-led innovation, whether in the craft traditions of skilled manual workers producing bespoke products, or backroom hobbyists producing their own novel products. The UK's major videogames industry grew initially from user-led innovations in software design using cheap, readily-available computer equipment.

## How Government Can Support Innovation and What More It Will Do
### Government procurement

3.10 Government is the single biggest customer in the UK economy. Government procurement amounts to around £150 billion every year on goods and services and Government has the potential itself to act as a lead market, pulling innovative products and services through from businesses. The Sainsbury review identified the need for Government to improve its performance in driving innovation through procurement.

3.11 In 2007, Government announced in *Transforming Government Procurement* a package of reforms to increase the level of procurement professionalism by improving skills within a more flexible and higher profile Government Procurement Service.[47] It also aimed to raise the status and standard of procurement practice within departments supported and driven by a smaller, higher calibre Office of Government Commerce which is conducting Procurement Capability Reviews of Departments. The increasing involvement of the private sector in the delivery of public services is helping to maintain and stimulate innovation in these areas. DeAnne Julius is currently leading a Review of the Public Service Industry which will look into these and wider issues around the involvement of the private sector in supplying services across Government. This work is due to report to BERR in Summer 2008.

3.12 The Sustainable Procurement Action Plan, published in March 2007, also identified ways of harnessing public sector purchasing power to make innovative and sustainable solutions more widely available and affordable to others and to help to deliver a low carbon economy.

## Case study

### MoD Innovation Strategy

Defence is increasingly underpinned by sophisticated innovation and the UK must apply innovation and world class technology in order to respond quickly and effectively to both existing and new military and counter-terrorism threats.

As part of a drive to achieve more innovation and pace in delivery of frontline capability, services and processes, MOD published an Innovation Strategy for the defence supply chain in December 2007. The Strategy is supported by a new business model that sets out an innovative and systemised approach to research covering four distinct stages: a) ideas capture, b) growth and development to permit a proper and mature assessment, c) demonstration, particularly in the operating environment and d) application in the frontline.

The MOD also runs several schemes aimed at delivering innovation. These include The Grand Challenge, a competition open to the UK science and technology community to develop an autonomous vehicle capable of detecting a range of military threats in an urban environment. In addition, the Competition of Ideas, a web-based scheme, set up to identify and take forward novel technologies relevant to defence, received over 400 proposals and resulted in 66 funded projects, a large percentage of which were from SMEs and academia.

3.13 To build on this work, each Government Department will include an Innovation Procurement Plan during 2008 as part of its commercial strategy, setting out how it will embed innovation in its procurement practices and seek to use innovative procurement mechanisms, based on the DIUS/OGC guidance included in *Finding and Procuring Innovative Solutions*[48]. These plans will include details of how Departments and the agencies they sponsor will seek to increase their procurement of innovative products and services, fulfil their commitments under existing initiatives such as the Small Business Research Initiative and how they will make use of innovative procurement mechanisms from 2009-10.

3.14 DIUS will work with the Technology Strategy Board, OGC and with Departments with experience in promoting innovation through procurement to support others to use their procurement power effectively in support of innovation.

3.15 DIUS and the CBI will work together to facilitate the interchange of innovation expertise between the public and private sector including the secondment of private sector exports into the public sector for the purpose of mentoring pro-innovation procurement.

3.16 Government Departments participating in SBRI agreed to a target of purchasing at least 2.5% of their R&D from SMEs. In 2006/07

Each Government Department will include an Innovation Procurement Plan as part of its commercial strategy, setting out how they will drive innovation through procurement and use innovative procurement practices.

DIUS will work with the Technology Strategy Board, OGC and with Departments with experience in promoting innovation through procurement to support others to use their procurement power effectively in support of innovation.

DIUS and the CBI will work together to facilitate the interchange of innovation expertise between the private sector and Government Departments, for example, through secondments and mentoring in innovative procurement and the design of services, products and processes.

DIUS will reform the SBRI, refocused on technology based research, prototyping this with the Ministry of Defence and the Department of Health and will extend the revised SBRI to all participating Departments by April 2009

the value of contracts made with SMEs was £136.9M, representing nearly 6% of the baseline budget.

3.17 DIUS and the Technology Strategy Board will work with Departments to address the deficiencies of SBRI identified by the Sainsbury review. The reformed SBRI will refocus SBRI projects on technology-based research (using a tightened definition of technology developed by HMT, the same as that used for assessing eligibility for the R&D Tax Credit) and be co-ordinated by the Technology Strategy Board acting as a central point for advertising tenders and providing expert advice to contracting departments. The Technology Strategy Board will also exercise an oversight function and ensure Departments participating in the SBRI meet their commitments. DIUS and the Technology Strategy Board will pilot the reformed SBRI with the Ministry of Defence and the Department of Health.

3.18 The report by the Commission for Environmental Markets and Economic Performance (CEMEP)[49] found that, in the context of the transition to a low carbon, resource efficient future, policy needed to be designed to enable business to respond in the most cost-effective way while also maximising the opportunities for wealth creation. The report stressed that policy should combine the standard instruments of regulation or market-based incentives, for example Forward Commitment Procurement, to internalise external costs while also providing direct support for innovation. DIUS will take forward this approach and extend it beyond environmental markets to also address other major challenges we face as a society.

3.19 DIUS will also work with BERR to ensure British businesses can benefit from the implementation of the European Commission's lead market initiative (see Chapter 6).

# Demanding Innovation

## Case study

### Renewable Energy

Renewable energy is an important element of the energy supply mix for environmental and diversity of supply reasons. There are major commercial opportunities in the UK and overseas for businesses that can deliver new and cost-effective renewable energy technologies. The Government has just signed up to ambitious targets for 2020 and will use a combination of policy instruments to meet these including:

• Market regulation to provide an incentive to invest in renewable energy (NFFO and ROCs)

• Planning policy which has an effect on where, how many and what types of renewable projects are deployed

• Public funding of underpinning basic research including a cross-Research Council programme on Energy

• Technology Strategy Board grant funding for companies to develop R&D based solutions

• The new Energy Technologies Institute

• The Environmental Transformation Fund for demonstration

• Supervision of major infrastructure projects (eg a feasibility study of the Severn Barrage)

DIUS will ensure, with the Technology Strategy Board, that relevant institutions from regulators to researchers, are brought together to identify and take advantage of new markets

3.20 The Technology Strategy Board's Innovation Platforms bring together Departments, business and academia to address a major societal challenge and to open up market opportunities to increase business investment in R&D and innovation.

3.21 Over the course of the next three years, the Technology Strategy Board will double its portfolio of Innovation Platforms, including developing technology demonstrators of innovative solutions. In the case of each Innovation Platform, the Technology Strategy Board will work with public and private sector stakeholders and the Government Department that "owns" the challenge to identify the levers to produce the desired response – in terms of the scale of the procurement opportunity, the speed and rigour of regulation or fiscal measures, and the value of any up-front investment – and then support the most innovative products and service ideas and bring them successfully to market.

## Case study

### Innovation Platform

The Low Carbon Vehicles Innovation Platform was launched by the Technology Strategy Board (TSB) in 2007 to accelerate the market introduction of low carbon road vehicles. The aim is both to maximise the benefit to UK business and to respond to the societal and business challenge of reducing transport $CO_2$ emissions. It coordinates Government support mechanisms for technology development within the wider market transformation context of the Low Carbon Transport Innovation Strategy. The first activity was a collaborative R&D programme with £20 million of support from the Department for Transport (DfT) and the TSB, focused on bringing forward vehicle technologies that could be viable candidates for commercialisation or fleet procurement over the next 5-7 years.

The next step is the TSB launch of a Low Carbon Vehicles Integrated Delivery Programme with an initial investment of £40 million jointly supported by the TSB, DfT and the Engineering and Physical sciences Research Council (EPSRC). It will provide greater co-ordination of activities from university research to future potential procurement opportunities, speeding up the time it takes to get low carbon vehicle technologies into the market place. Complementary funding to enhance the scope of the demonstration activity is under discussion with Regional Development Agencies & Devolved Administrations. Advantage West Midland's Board has identified the potential for up to £30 million of investment in this initiative subject to the regional economic benefits.

## Regulation

3.22 The role of regulation in relation to innovation is complex – it can either act as a barrier by creating additional costs or as a promoter of innovation through creating incentives to produce improved products and services. Frequently, it must deal with competing objectives such as facilitating experimentation while simultaneously protecting individuals from harms and risks. Substantial attention has been paid over recent years to making regulation smarter – through reducing the costs of compliance, focussing on the highest risks and giving more freedom to business to choose the ways in which it meets the outcomes desired. Much of this has helped regulation to become more pro-innovation.

3.23 There have also been some specific examples of recent reviews in which the role of regulation has been considered. The Commission on Environmental Markets and Economic Performance examined the ways in rising environmental standards can help improve economic performance and create new markets. It looked at how well designed environmental regulation can drive technology forward. And in the case of the water industry a review (the Cave Review) has recently been announced into questions surrounding competition and innovation. But there has been no general examination of the practical ways in which regulation should be framed and implemented in order to have the greatest effect on innovation and in turn the ways in which technological change affects overall regulatory responsibilities and powers.

## Regulation

The UK leads the world in the up-take of digital TV with over 85% of households already accessing digital television. Government is seeking to provide a policy and regulation lead which enables the provision of more channels and features for consumers and broadcasters whilst freeing up spectrum for other users and new markets. Innovation will be supported through the liberation of the spectrum used by analogue terrestrial television for new products and services such as, for example, mobile broadcasting and by enabling enhanced and interactive services to be developed.

DCMS and BERR, are working with Digital UK, Ofcom, broadcasters, businesses and consumer groups and coordinating internationally to ensure switchover happens smoothly.

3.24 The Government has concluded that it would be appropriate to draw together previous experience of the ways in which regulation can lead to more innovation in order to learn lessons and help frame future regulation. It proposes two specific actions. First DIUS, and the Better Regulation Executive in BERR will work with the Business Council for Britain and others to identify the lessons to be learned about the use of regulation to promote innovation.

3.25 Secondly, BERR and DIUS will jointly take forward discussions with regulators to share experience on how their activities can best promote innovation and draw on the support mechanisms which Government provides for innovation in business.

3.26 The Technology Strategy Board will advise Government on the opportunities which may arise from the adoption of EU regulations to stimulate business innovation (see Chapter 6)

DIUS and the Better Regulation Executive in BERR will work with the Business Council for Britain and others to identify how regulation may promote or hinder innovation.

DIUS and the Better Regulation Executive in BERR will use existing regulators' fora, to share experience on how their activities could promote innovation.

## Building an Innovative Consumer Base: A New Science & Society Strategy

3.27 The UK population places more confidence on science and technology to solve major global challenges than many other EU countries.

3.28 The Government is reviewing its vision and strategy for Science and Society. The Secretary of State have set out their aim to achieve "a society that is excited about science, values its importance to our economic and social well-being, feels confident in its use, and supports a representative, well-qualified scientific workforce".

3.29 This work will result in a strategy that will be published in the Autumn. The strategy will build on the current pro-science culture in the UK and seek to develop stronger relationships between the groups involved – society, science and policy – challenging them to align policies and work together on a shared agenda.

> DIUS will publish an agreed Science and Society strategy in the Autumn along with an implementation and delivery plan

# 4. Supporting Business Innovation

*Business is an engine of innovation, a generator of wealth and a driver of improved living standards. Government plays a critical role in guaranteeing the framework within which businesses can innovate and in providing direct support where the market fails.*

*The UK has significant strengths across all sectors of its economy and innovation performance is on an upwards trend. Strategic organisations like the Technology Strategy Board, RDAs, UK-IPO, ETI and NESTA as well as those in Scotland, Wales and Northern Ireland play important roles in driving innovation and coordinating government effort.*

*DIUS will continue to improve the environment for innovative businesses. It will expand the scale and range of knowledge exchange activities and institute innovation vouchers to introduce a new stream of businesses to the UK's knowledge base institutions. With BERR, DIUS will manage an escalator of financial support for all types of innovative businesses at all stages of their development and continue to improve the UK's intellectual property regime to reflect the changing face of innovation.*

## The Importance of Innovation for Business Success

4.1 Government's main task is to maintain framework conditions in which business can innovate with confidence and to correct market failures. The UK is a strong performer on innovation and ranks in the leading group of EU economies; manufacturing, services and creative industries are all internationally competitive. The Technology Strategy Board is well placed to support UK business in retaining a technological and innovative advantage over competitors, notably through its innovation platforms. We also possess a world class innovation infrastructure. However, accessing finance and managing intellectual property can be a problem for some innovative companies, and there is scope for Government to create a more integrated escalator of financial support for business.

## Where the UK Stands

Innovation and the UK economy

4.2 Britain is the world's 6th largest manufacturer. Manufacturing adds over £150 billion a year to the UK economy, accounting for around a seventh of total UK output and three-quarters of all business R&D. It generates over 50% of UK exports and directly employs almost three million people. It is an innovative sector, accounting for around three-quarters of all business R&D, and introducing new products and services into the economy. The UK sets the gold standard in areas such as aerospace, pharmaceuticals, food processing, high performance cars, and nanomaterials. We also have many prestigious design-led construction projects and the UK is famed for its iconic design.

4.3 Survey-based measures of private sector innovation show the overall rate of innovation in the UK to be around the European average. However, on traditional measures, the UK does not perform so well[50]. The UK is sixth in the G7 in terms of total R&D expenditure as a share of GDP and trends have been flat over the past decade. Measures of patent applications per head of population for the UK are lower than for major competitors.

4.4 Recent analysis has suggested that at least part of the gap is due to the sector mix of the economy, not under-investment in R&D by UK companies[51]. The combined service sectors account for around 75% of output in the UK[52] and other categories of investment in innovation are more important to them. Only a third of UK business spend on innovation is on R&D[53].

4.5 Britain's creative industries[54] are growing at twice the rate of other industries, contributing £60 billion to the UK economy. Two million people work in the creative industries or as creative professionals in other sectors. The creative industries are also a huge part of the UK's global reputation; a statement of cultural diversity; and a chance for many young people to achieve success.

4.6 Businesses change their management practices and business structures both as a means of capitalising on new products and services but also as an independent means to improve competitiveness. During the three year period 2004 to 2006, one third of business with 10 or more staff were engaged in these types of innovation.

4.7 Innovation also happens through the creation and growth of new firms; this is an essential ingredient of disruptive innovations that transform or create markets and provides the rationale for Government supporting the establishment and growth of smaller firms, as set out in the BERR Enterprise Strategy[55].

Access to finance

4.8 Availability of finance is critical to the UK's innovation system. Venture capital is often the most appropriate form of funding for innovative small and medium sized firms.

4.9 The UK's supply of finance to innovative firms has improved in recent years. Our venture capital (VC) industry, excluding management buy-outs and buy-ins, has doubled as a share of GDP between 1997 and 2004 but it is still only half that of the United States[56,57]. Business angels invested £29 million in 2005, up from £14 million in 2003. Although no comprehensive recent survey of business angel activity is available, it was estimated that in 2000 there were between 4,000 and 6,000 business angels in the UK, investing up to £1 billion annually[58].

4.10 Despite these signs of health, there is a systematic under-supply of risk capital in the £250,000 to £2 million range. Potential finance providers and investors often lack all the information needed to fully assess the risks and returns associated with a business proposal of this scale.

4.11 Weaknesses in a business' internal capacity and skill set to commercialise innovative products and services can be a disincentive to innovation.

### Innovation infrastructure

4.12 The World Bank rates the UK as one of the 10 best places for doing business internationally. The UK's innovation infrastructure, notably intellectual property (IP) systems and procedures, standards (BSI British Standards) and the National Measurement System (NMS) and its facilities are key contributors to this success.

4.13 The Gowers Review[59] examined the UK's IP framework and found it broadly fit for purpose, but also recommended strengthening enforcement of IP rights, reducing the costs of IP transactions and adjusting the balance and flexibility of rights for the digital age. There is evidence that SMEs in particular need to be more aware of IP.

4.14 BSI's catalogue of standards is responsible for £2.5 billion of GDP each year[60] and the NMS supports the development of new products through better measurement, enabling users to achieve annual increased profits of £712 million[61]. The National Physical Laboratory is one of the top three measurement laboratories internationally.

### Technology Strategy Board

Activities supported by the Technology Strategy Board include:

- Innovation Platforms foster developments across technologies in response to societal challenges

- Knowledge Transfer Networks promote the benefits to organisations of communicating their own ideas and learning from others

- Knowledge Transfer Partnerships help spread technical and business skills through projects in business undertaken by high calibre individuals

- Collaborative R&D projects to enable businesses and research communities to work together.

## How Government can Stimulate Innovation and What More It Will Do

### Support for business innovation

4.15 The Technology Strategy Board plays an important leadership role operating across all important sectors of the UK economy to stimulate innovation in those areas which offer the greatest scope for boosting UK growth and productivity. Over the next three years starting

April 2008, the Technology Strategy Board will develop and lead a strategic programme worth £1 billion, in partnership with the Research Councils and the Regional Development Agencies (RDA), to support technology and innovation activities for the benefit of UK business. This includes £180 million which will be earmarked by the RDAs and £120 million by the Research Councils to spend jointly on activities with the Technology Strategy Board.

## Case study

### Collaborative R&D

The Technology Strategy Board, set up to drive investment in business innovation, has invested in a collaborative research project that is addressing the problem of liquid crystal displays – such as those in watches, phones and laptops – going to waste. It is estimated that over 3 billion devices with LCD displays were manufactured in 2006 and environmentally acceptable disposal of the displays is a growing problem. Materials they contain are known to be persistent pollutants and in addition, valuable resources such as liquid crystals and short-supply metals such as indium are being lost. The project, called Reflated, is investigating ways of recycling and reusing these materials and working with industry to improve the recyclability of liquid crystal displays in future. The consortium of partners includes recyclers, technology developers, a specialist chemical processor and an engineering equipment manufacturer. In the early stages of the project a number of innovative processes have already been developed and are being scaled up and market tested.

4.16 Securing reliable, sustainable energy is a key Government priority. The Energy Technologies Institute (ETI), announced in the 2006 Budget, is a public-private partnership that brings together some of the world's biggest energy and engineering companies – BP, Caterpillar, EDF Energy, E.ON UK, Rolls-Royce and Shell. It will invest up to £110 million per year in low carbon technology development for at least the next 10 years. ETI will help to deliver UK's climate change goals by bringing more focus, ambition and collaboration to the UK's work in energy science and engineering.

4.17 Business support is also provided through the Regional Development Agencies (RDAs) who both deliver tailored business support products at a regional level and support a number of the Government's national programmes to stimulate innovation. Their key strength is their knowledge and understanding of their region and ability to address regional priorities.

4.18 Design is linked to business performance[62]. The Design Council and Regional Development Agencies (RDAs) have rolled out the Designing Demand service – a mentoring programme that uses design to transform business competitiveness. The programme has already benefited 1200 Small and Medium size Enterprises (SMEs) nationwide since 2002.

4.19 The Business Support Simplification Programme (BSSP) will make it easier for companies and entrepreneurs to understand and access government funding and advice to help start and grow their businesses. The 3,000+ schemes currently in operation will be reduced to approximately 100 by 2010. Business Links (managed by the RDAs) will become the primary access route for individuals and businesses seeking support.

4.20 R&D Tax Credits are a major Government incentive for business R&D. About £600 million is claimed annually by about 6,000 companies. Budget 2007 announced an increase in the rates of the relief from 150 to 175% for SMEs (EU approval for this increase is awaited) and from 125 to 130% for large companies to take effect from April 2008. The 2007 Finance Act included legislation to extend the SME scheme to companies with up to 500 employees, subject to EU approval.

## What Government will do

4.21 DIUS will champion a series of 'Innovation Collaborations'. This will include Innovation Platforms and Knowledge Transfer Partnerships. The Innovation Platform concept and the use of lead markets for innovative products and services will address major societal challenges. Over the course of the next three years, the Technology Strategy Board will double the number of Innovation Platforms to 10. When there are significant new opportunities for UK businesses, DIUS will ensure that all relevant institutions, from regulators to researchers and users are brought together to identify and take advantage of new

markets. In line with the Sainsbury Review, the Technology Strategy Board, RDAs and Research Councils are expanding Knowledge Transfer Partnerships (KTP) to double their number over the next three years and for the first time they will cover the service sectors. Shorter term KTPs and KTP opportunities from further education institutions will also be available from Autumn 2008.

4.22 The Government will encourage the development of Innovation Voucher whereby SMEs receive a voucher that can "buy" initial engagement with a knowledge base institution such as a higher or further education institution. Smaller, less well established businesses often do not understand or struggle to access the benefits of external knowledge and collaboration. This is counter to the perceived trend for more open and user-led models of innovation, where a significant proportion of innovative ideas originates from or is exploited outside the business.

## Case study

### Knowledge Transfer Partnerships

Breval Environmental Limited conceived the idea for a system that was capable of navigating a building's ventilation ductwork whilst applying a coating to the internal walls. The company recognised the potential benefits of such a system over conventional mechanical cleaning. For example, coatings may seal small leaks in older ducting, encapsulate hazardous contaminants or offer an antibacterial surface. However, as a building services contractor, Breval did not have the necessary expertise in-house to see the project through. Help came through a Knowledge Transfer Partnership (KTP), which provided the Company with access to the expertise in Bell College's School of Science and Technology. The benefits to the company include an innovative, patented remote-controlled system developed for cleaning and coating dirty and contaminated ventilation systems in buildings.

Helping Breval to develop product design, development and prototype manufacturing capabilities and break into a new market area proved a challenging yet rewarding experience for the KTP Associate. He applied and enhanced his technical know-how, skilfully using computer-aided engineering software to model the vehicle and control station.

Involvement in the design, development and testing of a new product provided staff at the College involved in engineering design with invaluable experience with case study material generated now incorporated into various undergraduate courses. Experience from the project will also feed into ongoing research into ductwork performance.

4.23 Correctly implemented, vouchers could potentially:

• overcome cultural or social barriers to engage with the knowledge base;

• help with the costs of innovation for SMEs;

• provide a more market-based mechanism for allocating some knowledge transfer resources to HEIs; and

• incentivise first-time engagement with the business support system.

4.24 A number of voucher schemes are in operation both regionally and internationally. Government's ambition is to increase the provision of vouchers over the next three years to meet business needs in line with regional priorities and within the BSSP framework. Over the English regions, at least 500 businesses will be given a voucher to work with a knowledge base institution of their choice, with the aspiration that this would increase to at least 1000 per year by 2011 as the vouchers were demonstrated to be effective for businesses. Given that the existing voucher scheme in the West Midlands provides vouchers with a value of £3,000, this is likely to involve an investment of at least £3 million to help first collaborations between SMEs and the knowledge base.

4.25 Innovation in the service sector often has a shorter time from conception to implementation and can become obsolete more quickly. Although frequently based on technology, such as IT, innovation in services frequently comes from identifying new applications of technologies or integrating them into business models and processes. However, innovation in services can have an impact across the wider economy. For example, recent innovations in logistics have resulted in significant innovation in the manufacturing

sector through enabling business models with a higher degree of supplier integration. In order to better understand innovation in the service sector, DIUS will continue to work with BERR, the Technology Strategy Board and NESTA to investigate the issues faced by service sectors such as internet services, retail, logistics, environmental services, and construction.

> **DIUS and the Technology Strategy Board working with partners will take forward the Sainsbury recommendation to double the number of Knowledge Transfer Partnerships, increasing their flexibility and applicability to a range of educational institutions including FE colleges.**
>
> **Over the English regions, at least 500 businesses will be given an innovation voucher to work with a knowledge base institution of their choice, with the aspiration that this would increase to at least 1000 per year by 2011 as the vouchers were demonstrated to be effective for businesses. This is expected to mean an investment of at least £3 million to initiate collaborations between SMEs and the knowledge base.**
>
> **DIUS will continue to work with BERR, Technology Strategy Board and NESTA to investigate the issues faced by particular service sectors.**

4.26 The Technology Strategy Board will also link its work on technology roadmaps with Defra's product roadmaps for the high environmental impact areas of transport, home and food.

# Supporting Business Innovation

The Technology Strategy Board will bring forward five new Innovation Platforms over the next three years including developing technology demonstrators to show innovative solutions in action.

DIUS and the Technology Strategy Board working with partners will take forward the Sainsbury recommendation to double the number of Knowledge Transfer Partnerships, increasing their flexibility and applicability to a range of educational institutions including FE colleges.

Over the English regions, at least 500 businesses will be given an innovation voucher to work with a knowledge base institution of their choice, with the aspiration that this would increase to at least 1000 per year by 2011 as the vouchers were demonstrated to be effective for businesses. This is expected to mean an investment of at least £3 million to initiate collaborations between SMEs and the knowledge base.

DIUS will continue to work with BERR, Technology Strategy Board and NESTA to investigate the issues faced by particular service sectors.

### Access to finance

4.27 The Government acts both to provide strong supply side support where there is evidence of market failure and to support businesses seeking to make themselves investment-ready.

4.28 Government has improved access to debt finance through the Small Firms Loan Guarantee where a business has a debt-appropriate proposition but does not have the collateral or track record to secure a loan. Since 1981, around 100,000 loans valued at £5 billion have been guaranteed.

4.29 Government equity funds have been established to stimulate equity and risk capital markets. Enterprise Capital Funds (ECF) invest a mix of private and public money in small high growth businesses that are seeking up to £2 million in risk capital. The Government has now committed over £141 million to ECF funding with a further £150 million earmarked for future funds over the next 3 years.

4.30 The Government also ensures that the tax system provides an additional incentive for investment in early stage and growth businesses through the Enterprise Investment Scheme (EIS) and Venture Capital Trusts (VCTs). Since its inception, the Enterprise Investment Scheme (EIS) has raised over £6.1 billion and invested in over 14,000 small, high-risk companies, while Venture Capital Trusts (VCTs) have invested over £3.2 billion in over 1,400 companies.

### What Government will do

4.31 The Government will build an escalator of financial support for innovative businesses at different stages of their growth. DIUS and the RDAs want to do more to help innovative businesses obtain appropriate finance. In partnership with stakeholders, DIUS will therefore lead work to deliver the recommendations of the Sainsbury review. The range of financial support programmes will be grouped together under the term "Innovation finance". In addition, DIUS aims to ensure that there are possible sources for the funding innovative businesses need at all stages of their growth and set out clearly how to obtain it in a guide to innovation finance based on the Business Link "No Nonsense Guide" on access to finance.

4.32 DIUS will take forward the Sainsbury Review recommendation to develop a nationally agreed proof of concept specification that links funding, access to facilities and mentoring. Over Spring/Summer 2008, views will be sought on the specification including the type of activity that should be supported, the timescales over which support is needed, the most appropriate form of support and the most effective delivery model, taking into account national and regional priorities.

> DIUS will work to ensure appropriate finance is available for all innovative businesses at all stages of their growth. This will be set out clearly in a "guide to innovation finance" based on the "No Nonsense Guide" on access to finance.

> DIUS will take forward the Sainsbury Review recommendation to develop a national proof of concept specification to be delivered by the RDAs, which will provide access to facilities and have a strong focus on investor readiness.

### Support for the UK's innovation infrastructure

4.33 Standardisation is a vital component of the innovation system, enabling the pull-through of products, services and processes into the market. It stimulates and supports demand and supply by providing confidence to consumers and reassurance to investors. Targeted application of standards to new and emerging technologies can accelerate and extend the application of innovative activity[63].

4.34 DIUS invests £60 million each year to make measurement more accurate for UK industry. The measurement programmes will increasingly focus on meeting the needs of business for technological innovation and maximising support for new high-value products and services.

4.35 As noted by the Gowers report, successful translation of creativity, ideas, insights and reputations into value is one of the critical determinants of our prosperity. The Intellectual Property system enables businesses to capture value from innovation. Beyond traditional concerns with the legal framework, Government's role is to make sure this process of value creation is working as well as it can. To this end:

- DIUS is examining whether better reporting of intangible assets such as IP by companies can help them secure finance

- The UK has led efforts to reduce backlogs at the European Patent Office and to improve the governance of the World Intellectual Property Organization, which is increasingly important to the IP system

- Patents rules have been overhauled and obtaining a UK trade mark has been made simpler, and

- The UK-IPO has begun to update the UK copyright framework for the digital age. It has already implemented a number of the Gowers report recommendations and is consulting on others including "format-shifting" and education and research exemptions.

### What Government will do

4.36 Standards are used to promote trust in services, both by improving consumer confidence in the quality of the service and by supporting the technology that underpins delivery of e-services and security of transactions. BSI will undertake an analysis of the role of standards within the service sector and will publish a strategy by April 2009. DIUS will work to promote British Standards in overseas markets.

4.37 An emerging field for standardisation is the area of innovation management. The original standard providing guidance to companies for managing innovation was first published in 2000 (BS 7000-1). This is being revised based on research within innovative companies to encapsulate best practice in this field. BSI will publish a revised standard on the management of innovation for April 2009.

4.38 DIUS will produce technology roadmaps for the NMS Programmes and publish a new strategic plan to identify and address the metrology barriers to innovation

4.39 Bringing about the best use of Intellectual Property in the economy will become central to the purpose of the UK-IPO. This will require a systematic economic understanding of how IP is used in the economy. The UK-IPO will establish a research programme to look at the economic evidence base on intellectual property and innovation, including the impact of new models of open and user-led innovation on the existing IP regime. In addition, the new Strategic Advisory Board on Intellectual Property will have an annual budget of £500,000 for research into IP-related policy issues.

4.40 Government's business support network will be used to promote an IP awareness-raising programme. By the summer of 2009, all UKTI export and Business Link advisors will receive training from the UK-IPO in advising businesses on IP management. The training will also be available in Scotland, Wales and Northern Ireland.

4.41 Government is committed to making IP transactions more straightforward and affordable. Reducing the cost to business of applying for registered rights such as patents and trademarks remains a priority for UK-IPO. UK-IPO will develop with stakeholders an online business-to-business licensing resource, that will reduce the cost to small businesses of IP collaborations.

BSI will undertake an analysis of the role of standards within the service sector and will publish a strategy.

BSI will publish a revised standard on the management of innovation for April 2009

DIUS will produce technology roadmaps for the NMS Programmes and publish a new strategic plan to identify and address the metrology barriers to innovation

The UK-IPO will examine whether there is a role for Government in helping small firms obtain investment through better reporting of their intangible assets, by the end of 2008.

By the summer of 2009 all UKTI export and Business Link advisors will receive training from the UK-IPO in advising businesses on IP management. UK-IPO will provide online support to help small business exploit their IP through licensing and other means which are increasingly important to innovative business. This network will be used to promote an awareness-raising programme on the importance and changing nature of intellectual property.

# 5. A Strong and Innovative Research Base

*A world-class research base is an important component of the UK's innovation infrastructure. Alongside other sources of knowledge like large companies, SMEs and users, it drives the creation of new ideas, some of which have potential to deliver significant economic and social benefits.*

*Working with the Research Councils and the Technology Strategy Board, DIUS will build on the UK's current impressive performance on research to broaden the traditional knowledge exchange agenda to encompass new disciplines, new sectors, new businesses and those who work in the development and delivery of public services.*

## The Importance of a Strong Research Base

5.1 The rationale for the Government's investment in the research base was set out in 2004 in the ten year Science and Innovation Investment Framework.[64]

*"Harnessing innovation in Britain is key to improving the country's future wealth creation prospects. For the UK economy to succeed in generating growth through productivity and employment in the coming decade, it must invest more strongly than in the past in its knowledge base and translate this knowledge more effectively into business and public service*
*innovation. The Government's ambition, shared with its partners in the private and not-for-profit sectors, is for the UK to be a key knowledge hub in the global economy, with a reputation not only for outstanding scientific and technological discovery, but also as a world leader in turning that knowledge into new products and services. At the core of the UK's knowledge base is its research and development (R&D) capacity, in the public and private sectors, which enables it to create, absorb and deploy new ideas rapidly."*

5.2 World-class research in the UK is crucial to maintaining economic prosperity and responding to the challenges and opportunities of globalisation. Research in universities and Government research laboratories is not the only source of knowledge creation but it is an important part of our innovation ecosystem.

5.3 In the global knowledge economy the UK's competitive advantage relies on the ingenuity and capabilities of our population and requires an innovative and enterprising culture to capitalise on opportunities. Our strengths in the aerospace and pharmaceuticals sectors are a good example of this. Lord Sainsbury commented:[65]

*"In today's global economy, investment in science and innovation is not an intellectual luxury for a developed country, but an economic and social necessity, and a key part of any strategy for economic success."*

5.4 Investment in the research base should drive innovation in the following five ways:

- Qualified people – highly skilled people trained within the research environment are in high demand in businesses across every sector from pharmaceuticals to finance.

- Improved products and processes – research outcomes help businesses and public services create new and better products and more effective and efficient processes.

- Attracting investment – major businesses from around the globe making R&D investments in the UK to gain access to our research base and its extraordinarily talented people.

- New businesses – ideas sparked from research leading to new, exciting commercial opportunities that sustain our knowledge economy, such as through spin out companies.

- Improved public policy – research adding to the evidence base and bringing about more effective policy making – from health care to flood defences, transport to food safety.

## Where the UK Stands
### Research performance statistics

5.5 The quality of the UK's research is world renowned. Our share of the top 1% of cited papers in peer-reviewed journals is second only to the United States and we lead the G8 on science productivity and efficiency measures.

5.6 The Government has delivered a major increase in funding for research and is committed to continue with this increase. By 2010/11 Government investment in the research base will have risen to almost £4 billion a year. According to Cancer Research UK, the UK is spending more per capita on cancer research than any other country in Europe.

5.7 Yet at the same time, other countries are also investing in research and becoming attractive to globally mobile R&D investors. The emerging economies in particular are likely to challenge us for our position in the future – and in fact are already in a position to deliver world class research and exploitation. China claims to have already pushed the UK into 3rd place in terms of the number of scientific papers produced (though citation rates are relatively low). And it is not just China and India who are in the ascendant – countries in the Middle East are increasingly investing in research

### Universities' track record on business and user collaboration

5.8 In recent years, there has been a culture shift in UK universities as the translation of research and business engagement has shifted from being a minor sideline to a core part of a university's mission.

5.9 Systematic information on various forms of Higher Education and business interaction show an upwards trend for most indicators. Increasing numbers of university spin-out companies are making their way onto the stock market and a recent venture capital report noted that there are now over 590 university spin-out companies in the UK which attract approximately 12% of the UK's substantial venture capital finance.[66]

**Level of incentives for engagement with business and the community**
(% levels of incentives)

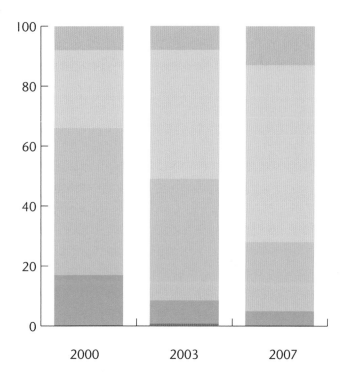

5) Strong positive signals given to all staff to encourage appropriate levels of industrial collaboration. Incentive procedures well established and clearly understood and applied.

4) Between 3 and 5

3) Some incentives in place, but with some barriers remaining. Typically policy may be generally supportive but there is a lack of understanding across the institution. Promotions committees still take a narrow focus on research even though guidance suggests industrial collaboration is valued equally.

2) Between 1 and 3

1) Barriers outweigh any incentives offered. General corporate culture is focused on internal activities and narrow interpretation of teaching and research. Collaboration with business seen by staff as detrimental to career progression.

5.10 In addition, universities are now increasingly making economic impact a core part of their mission, and accordingly providing incentives (for example promotion assessment) to researchers to take part in this activity. The chart shows how there has been a clear increase in positive incentives for staff in this area.

## How Government can Support Innovation and What More It Will Do

### Research funding for the public good

5.11 There is a well understood rationale for Government investment in research – particularly fundamental research. Left to its own devices, the private sector will under invest in this area, since the benefits of such research are spread widely and not easily captured by the original investor in the research. Public funding of research is a long term investment by the Government in the innovation potential of the country.

5.12 The Government supports research through the "dual support" system. Strategic funding is provided via a block grant. In England this funding comes from DIUS and is channelled through the Higher Education Funding Council for England (HEFCE); parallel arrangements operate in the Devolved Administrations. In addition, DIUS funds the Research Councils through the Science Budget, and they in turn fund research across the UK on a project basis. Since 1997 the ring-fenced Science Budget has increased from £1.3 billion to £3.4 billion per annum. It is due to increase further over the next few years. Taken together, DIUS now invests £6 billion a year through the dual support system to foster a financially sustainable research base.

5.13 Block grant funding provides stability and a strategic resource that universities can invest to develop research areas according to their priorities, including new and emerging areas. Research Council funding provides vigorous competition on a project basis.

The two combine to drive excellence in the research base with flexibility to respond to changes and opportunities.

DIUS research programmes

*Cross-research council programmes on grand challenges*

5.14 The research base has the potential to have a major impact on the key public policy challenges currently facing the UK. The Science Budget is supporting a number of ambitious cross-council programmes which are being coordinated by Research Councils UK. These programmes will involve new ways of multi-disciplinary working, combining resources from a range of bodies to address the following challenges:

• Energy: the Research Councils' Energy Programme brings together energy-related research and training across the Councils to address the vital international issues of climate change and security of energy supply.

• Living With Environmental Change (LWEC): LWEC is an interdisciplinary research and policy partnership programme to increase resilience to – and reduce costs of – environmental change, addressing the associated pressures on natural resources, ecosystem services, economic growth and social progress.

• Global Threats to Security: this programme will integrate research in crime, terrorism, environmental stress and global poverty, to address causes of threats to security, their detection, and possible interventions to prevent harm.

• Ageing – lifelong health and wellbeing: this initiative will establish new interdisciplinary research centres targeting the major determinants of health and wellbeing at every stage of life, reducing dependency in later life.

5.15 These programmes are also being run in conjunction with the business community. For example the Energy programme will work with the Energy Technologies Institute (ETI) and Technology Strategy Board and the LWEC programme aims to work with at least 9 Government Departments and the Regional Development Agencies.

*Medical Research*

5.16 The allocation of the Science Budget significantly increases the funding available for medical research, training and knowledge transfer. In particular, the allocation will provide additional funding for public health and translational research, in line with the recommendations of the Cooksey Review.[67]

5.17 DIUS is part funding the new Office for the Strategic Co-ordination of Health Research (OSCHR). The aim of OSCHR is to work with the Medical Research Council (MRC) and Department of Health to facilitate more effective translation of health research into health and economic benefits to the UK.

5.18 A specific MRC allocation will, together with funding from the Department of Health, form a single health research budget for OSCHR. OSCHR's budget will rise to £1.7 billion per annum by 2010-11.

Putting research on a sustainable footing

5.19 Over the last decade the Government has provided successive rounds of capital funding through programmes like the Science Research Investment Fund to address the backlog of investment in the research base. Additionally, we have sought to put research on a firmer footing going forwards by introducing a new methodology[68] for costing research and by making a commitment to move towards paying the full economic costs (FEC) of research.

We have also announced that the temporary SRIF programme will be replaced by a permanent capital funding stream – the Research Capital Investment Fund. This will provide an ongoing stream of research capital to institutions engaged in research.

5.20 RCUK will be carrying out a post-implementation review of FEC, to evaluate the benefits so far and establish lessons for the future.

### Science and innovation campuses

5.21 The Government is fully committed to the development of both the Harwell and Daresbury sites as Science and Innovation Campuses, as outlined in the Government's Ten Year Science and Innovation Investment Framework Next Steps document.[69]

5.22 The Government's vision for the Science and Innovation Campuses is that they should be places where new collaborative approaches to research, innovation and learning are developed. They will be environments where scientists from a wide range of disciplines can work in a mutually supportive and cohesive manner. The Campuses will be prime locations for the international R&D sector, and will contribute to the development of the UK's internationally renowned scientific and high-technology skills base. Public sector organisations will work alongside businesses exploiting research to develop and profit from innovative products and services. Small, medium and large public and private organisations can also co-locate to their mutual benefit.

5.23 In December 2007 the Prime Minister announced Government's support for the intention to create the UK Centre for Medical Research and Innovation. The Centre aims to be Europe's leading centre for medical research. This is a collaboration between the Medical Research Council, Cancer Research UK, The Wellcome Trust and University College London.

The Centre is expected to be ready by the end of 2013.

### Driving up the impact of research

5.24 The Science Budget Allocations from the Comprehensive Spending Review 2007 settlement saw the Government place the strongest emphasis ever on economic impact.

5.25 The Government supports the exploitation of research through setting the right frameworks and encouraging a culture of interaction between researchers and users:

* The Research Councils have publicly committed to driving up the economic impact of the research they fund.

* The Government has strengthened the capacity in Higher Education Institutions in England and Wales to take part in knowledge transfer and business engagement through the Higher Education Innovation Fund (HEIF). This fund, now a permanent part of the University funding landscape, will increase to £150m per year by 2010/11. Funding will be allocated entirely through a formula and the benefits distributed more widely in line with Lord Sainsbury's recommendations.[70]

* Other measures include:

– QR block grant – HEFCE have introduced a dedicated element which reflects how well institutions attract business research funding (£60m).

– Research Assessment Exercise – the recent review has considered business aspects, including incentives for applied, practice-based and interdisciplinary research, and user views.

– Public Sector Research Exploitation Fund (PSRE) – the latest round of the Fund (draw down of which will be available from July

2008) has included a requirement for co-funding from other organisations, in line with Lord Sainsbury's recommendation.

— Research Council / Technology Strategy Board / RDA collaboration – Research Councils have committed £120 million and RDAs £180 million to collaborative work with the Technology Strategy Board over the next three years. This builds on a recommendation made by Lord Sainsbury in his review.

## Government as a user of research

5.26 Government policy-making needs to be underpinned by robust scientific evidence and long-term thinking; maintaining and analysing the evidence base is a critical to developing Government's strategies and policies and ensuring effective delivery of public services. The research base is a key driver of Government and public sector innovation.

5.27 All Government Departments now draw on the research base to inform policy development with most having Chief Scientific Advisers, usually drawn from academia. DIUS has the ministerial lead for Science and houses the Government Office for Science (GO-Science). GO-Science is led by the Government Chief Scientific Adviser, who has overall responsibility for championing and improving scientific advice to support better policy making across Government. GO-Science also runs the Foresight Programme which is a major driver of innovation in policy making across Government.

5.28 In the Summer of 2008 GO-Science will be publishing its forward programme along with a consolidated set of policies and guidance. This will bring together Government's science policy and guidance into one place, ensuring transparency and making it simpler for Government Departments to access science guidance and support.

## Delivering the Sainsbury agenda

5.29 DIUS and its partners have made good progress on delivering the recommendations outlined in Lord Sainsbury's review. Six months on, over 20 recommendations have been fully implemented.[71] In particular, HEIF is to be allocated wholly by formula, specific knowledge transfer targets have been agreed for each Research Council (and published in their Delivery Plans) and the next round of the Public Sector Research Establishment Fund will require co-funding from other organisations.

## Case study

### Impact of research

A joint project between the Department of Landscape at The University of Sheffield, and Timberplay aims to revolutionise playground environments and promote the benefits of play in more "natural" environments. This helps support the Government's Children's Plan which places an emphasis on children's ability to play. Innovation in the design of play spaces will be stimulated by the transfer of knowledge and the skills of landscape design to the company. Public sector funding for the project comes from the Arts and Humanities Research Council (AHRC), ESRC and the Technology Strategy Board.

# A Strong and Innovative Research Base

## Case study

### Molecular diagnostic tools help fight infectious diseases.

The Biochip project,[72] a substantial research initiative to develop diagnostic viral microarray technology for detection of about 600 viral pathogens, is one of the recommendations of the Foresight project on The Detection and Identification of Infectious Diseases[73] launched in April 2006. It is led by Defra's Central Science Laboratory (CSL) and supported by Defra's Chief Scientific Adviser. It is a collaboration between CSL, the Centre for Environment, Fisheries & Aquaculture Science, the Veterinary Laboratories Agency, the Institute of Animal Health, the Health Protection Agency and the Royal Veterinary College. Uniquely, the project draws together diverse expertise to develop methods for early diagnosis of infectious viral pathogens across the animal, plant, bee and fish sectors. The project also aims to improve detection of newly emerging pathogenic threats.

### Broadening the knowledge exchange agenda

5.30 Government will look to broaden and strengthen knowledge transfer activity in particular academic disciplines, such as Arts and Humanities, or particular business sectors such as the creative industries (in line with the Creative Economy Programme). DIUS will commission studies into economic impact, looking at good practice from around the world and identifying ways to improve practice in the UK.

### Intellectual property and universities

5.31 UK- IPO will continue to support the development of the 'Lambert' online toolkit of model university-business licensing agreements, which cuts the cost and complexity of IP transactions. DIUS is exploring better metrics to improve our understanding, and how we can bring all our institutions up to the level of the best in exploiting IP.

5.32 One area that attracts significant debate is the way in which universities should be expected to use the Intellectual Property they develop: for example, what should be the balance between universities reaping the fruits of their own labour and delivering wider benefits? DIUS has commissioned the Vice Chancellor of Lancaster University, Paul Wellings, to lead a study into how universities should manage IP for their own benefit and for the benefit of the wider economy.

### A new Innovation Index and an Innovation Research Centre

5.33 R&D is important for innovation in some sectors of the Economy, and is therefore crucial for economic growth. The Government therefore supports it with measures such as the R&D tax credit and in 2004, set itself an ambition for R&D spending to reach 2.5 % of GDP by 2014.

5.34 However, developing this strategy has highlighted areas where the existing body of knowledge needs to be developed and the need for better measures – a recurrent theme in the workshops that informed the development of this strategy. We need a better understanding of how innovation takes place and its economic and social value, the barriers to innovation, and the actions that businesses, service providers and Government can take to overcome them. We need to understand which actions are effective and in what context. And we need this knowledge freely available and widely understood throughout policy making, business and public service communities. The accompanying evidence document identifies long-term priorities for improvement.

DIUS will maintain the growing investment in UK science and will broaden knowledge exchange between the research base and businesses into the arts and humanities and service sectors such as the creative industries.

The UK-IPO will continue to develop the "Lambert" online toolkit of model university-business licensing agreements which cuts the cost and complexity of IP transactions.

DIUS has commissioned a study to look at how universities should manage IP for their own benefit and for the benefit of the wider economy.

5.35 NESTA will develop a new Innovation Index to measure UK innovation drawing on input and expertise from partners such as the ONS, DIUS, BERR, TSB, AIM, the Design Council, CBI and others. A pilot index will be published in 2009 with a fuller system in place by 2010.

5.36 The creation of an Index will enable NESTA to:

• Identify gaps in current measures.

• Embed existing innovation measures in a broader portfolio of other indicators that better reflect innovation outcomes and activities across the UK's economy and society.

• Improve our understanding of service sector, user-led and public sector innovation.

• Build on measures that innovative firms and their investors find useful.

5.37 DIUS, NESTA, ESRC and the Technology Strategy Board will create an Innovation Research Centre to ensure a steady supply of high quality innovation research into the UK innovation policy community. The centre will act as a focal point for research on innovation, co-ordinating

contributions from academia, Government and policy research centres as well as developing links with international sources of expertise in this area, such as the OECD.

5.38 The Government will continue to carry out and fund research into innovation, including commissioning of research into the economic benefits of the creative industries, as announced in Creative Britain, the Government's strategy for the creative industries.[74]

5.39 DIUS and BERR will also continue to work with other countries through OECD and EU processes to strengthen the framework for internationally comparable statistics and sharing experiences of policies and practice. The UK, for example, is leading a project with eight other countries modelling the relationship between innovation and productivity. The OECD intend to produce an innovation strategy in 2010. We will use this opportunity to argue for broadening international frameworks to incorporate better the roles of creativity and design, the role of users and innovation in public services.

**NESTA will develop an Innovation Index to measure UK innovation drawing on input and expertise from partners such as the ONS, DIUS, BERR, TSB, AIM, the CBI and others. A pilot index will be published in 2009 with a fuller system in place by 2010.**

**DIUS, NESTA, ESRC and the Technology Strategy Board will create an Innovation Research Centre to ensure a steady supply of high quality innovation research into the UK innovation policy community.**

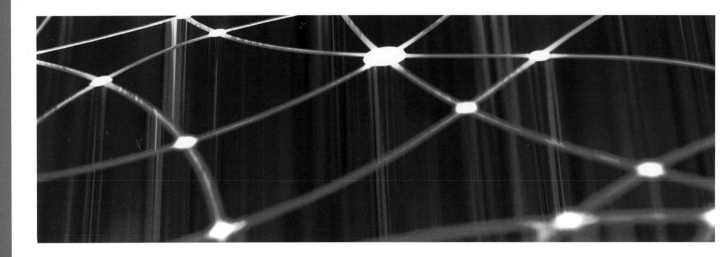

# 6. International Innovation

*Innovation is increasingly an international endeavour. Businesses are internationalising their R&D, supply chains and customer bases and adopting "open innovation" models. Like the ideas that they create and use, the people who drive innovation are also increasingly mobile, as is the finance that supports innovators.*

*The Government is committed to making the UK one of the most attractive places in the world for mobile R&D intensive businesses to invest. Its research base promotes collaboration for excellence irrespective of national borders and our open economy facilitates the internationalisation of high-tech businesses. However, international innovation competition is intensifying, spurred on by increasing investment by emerging economies.*

*DIUS will build on the UK's strengths in scientific and technological research collaboration to ensure that the UK is well-positioned to maximise its benefit from global innovation. DIUS will produce an international strategy that reflects the shifting geography of innovation, campaign to improve international intellectual property law and help businesses exploit IP internationally. Finally, it will seek deeper involvement with European initiatives to boost research and build access to Europe-wide lead markets for UK businesses.*

## The International Dimension of UK Innovation Policy

6.1 Science and innovation are international endeavours. Businesses are internationalising their R&D, supply chains and customer bases and adopting "open innovation" models of value creation. Scientists, engineers and entrepreneurs are increasingly mobile. From Shanghai to San Paulo, Hyderabad to Helsinki, new entrants are disrupting established patterns of innovation as they seek out opportunities.

6.2 The evidence base supporting the importance of international links is growing. Many of the major policy challenges identified for the coming decades arise from global problems that will require global collaborations to deliver solutions. Organisations need to attain "critical mass" in order effectively to tackle the big challenges.

6.3 The UK is in a good position. The strength of our research base, coupled with widespread use of English throughout the world and the openness both of our economy and academic recruitment, make the UK an attractive partner and location for internationally mobile investors. The UK has a higher share of foreign-born highly skilled persons than most of its EU neighbours including France and Germany[74]. In terms of highly skilled immigrants from outside the OECD, the UK boasts a larger share of those than most other EU countries. Furthermore, the UK plays a host to a large number of foreign PhD students.

6.4 A good indicator of the quantity of international links is the co-authorship of scientific publications. The percentage of UK papers written with an international co-author rose from 29% to 40% between 1996-2000 and 2001-2005 – the largest increase of any country in a recent study.[75]

6.5 The same bibliometric data show that international collaboration has a positive impact on the quality of science as measured by citation analysis. That is, publications resulting from international collaboration are more widely recognised in the work of peers than those which do not.

6.6 The UK research base is one of the most cosmopolitan in the world. In 2005-2006, 37% of doctoral science, technology, engineering and mathematics students and about 20% of academic staff came from overseas.

6.7 However we cannot afford to relax. In the face of growing competition we need to ensure that the science-driven, arms-length system which underpins our success nationally and internationally is able to adapt to the challenges of the changing global environment. We should be seeking to influence the shaping of international demand for innovative products, ensuring the UK benefits, as we are seeking to do at national level. It is vital that we also proactively promote the UK internationally on the basis of its science, education and innovation strength.

6.8 Highly skilled migrants contribute to reducing the cost of innovation for a country, primarily by saving it the cost of training that was incurred by the immigrants' sending countries and by reducing the cost of entry to foreign and international knowledge networks.[76] Moreover, they often play an important role in improving the ability of a country to respond to fluctuations in the supply and demand for certain skills in the local labour market.[77] In some of the sciences and in engineering the enrolment of local students has only recently begun to rise but rapid technological change and the emergence of new knowledge fields create new demands for various types of skills.

International R&D

6.9 For many of the same reasons identified above, the UK is an attractive place for businesses to undertake R&D. The UK is ranked by OECD as the fifth most attractive location for foreign-funded R&D[78] and was recently recognised as an "Innovation Leader" in the 2007 edition of the European Innovation Scoreboard.[79]

6.10 Total R&D expenditure by affiliates of foreign companies increased by more than 40% in the UK for the period 1994-2004. In the UK, this foreign investment (in 2004) accounted for 40% of the total R&D expenditure performed in the business sector, a much higher proportion than most other European countries.

EU dimension

6.11 The importance of innovation to the EU economic reform process and to other (e.g. environmental and social) shared European goals has steadily increased since the Lisbon summit in 2000. In March 2005, the Spring European Council agreed to re-launch the Lisbon Strategy to focus sharply on the key priorities of jobs and growth. Against this background the Government published its first National Reform Programme (NRP) in October 2005, setting out priority areas for national economic reform and policy commitments to support that reform.[80]

6.12 The main aim of the European R&D Framework Programmes (FPs) is to improve the competitiveness of European businesses and the focus of much of the Programme is on innovation-oriented, user-led collaborative research. The engagement of business is therefore crucial to a successful outcome.

6.13 While there have been widespread concerns regarding the relatively low level of business participation in FP6, the results for the UK are of particular concern in comparison to other large Member States.

6.14 With the new seven year spending programme, FP7, underway, further attention has been given to the concept of a European Research Area – often described as a single market for ideas or as a "fifth freedom of knowledge". This concept takes EU research and innovation policy well beyond the narrow confines of the FP, which represents less than 10% of public research funding in the EU, and aims to use the remaining ninety plus

per cent (ie the spending by Member States) in a more effective and coordinated way. As EU increases in spending outstrip those at national level, it will be increasingly important for the UK to maintain its influence over the design of EU research and innovation policies and programmes.

6.15 As a high proportion of legislation enacted in the UK flows from the EU, it is important that UK enterprises have the opportunity to develop innovative solutions to underpin compliance, for example in the environmental area.

## How Government Can Support Innovation and What More It Will Do
UKTI refocusing on high tech and R&D intensive business

6.16 UK Trade & Investment (UKTI) has the lead within Government for delivering international trade development and inward investment services for business and also for marketing the UK business offer internationally.

6.17 UKTI is rolling out business-led UK marketing strategies aimed at overseas buyers and potential investors for the Financial Services, ICT, Life Sciences, Creative and Energy sectors. These are sectors of high business innovation (for example the pioneering development of the UK's Islamic banking

**Engagement in FP6 (2002-2006) by sector (%)**[81]

| Category | UK | Germany | France |
| --- | --- | --- | --- |
| Higher Education | 56 | 32 | 19 |
| Industry | 19 | 26 | 24 |
| Research Centres | 14 | 31 | 40 |
| Others | 11 | 11 | 17 |

offer). The strategies require the development of new partnerships between business and Government to deliver a collective marketing effort. The strategies will speak as much to the overseas customer of UK products and services as they will to the potential investors looking for a new location, for partners or for joint ventures. New strategies around the UK offering for Climate Change and Advanced Engineering will be developed during 2008.

## UK Global and Science Innovation Forum (GSIF)

6.18 The Global Science and Innovation Forum (GSIF) chaired by the Government's Chief Scientific Advisor and comprising a wide range of Government departments and key stakeholders is implementing its strategy. The strategy aims to provide an overarching framework to enable better coordination and prioritisation between the various organisations promoting UK science and innovation overseas.

The strategy is based on four priority areas:

- research excellence – through strengthened international collaborations and attracting the best researchers to the UK;

- excellence in innovation – through UK businesses accessing international science and by attracting international R&D investments to the UK;

- global influence – by using international science to underpin foreign policy and as a tool to promote bilateral partnerships; and

- development – using research and innovation to meet international development goals.

6.19 In recognition of the increasing importance of emerging economies, GSIF has developed bilateral engagements through Government-to-Government policy dialogue platforms e.g. the UK-India Science and Innovation Council, and

## Case study

### UKTI'S R&D programme

This UKTI programme targets overseas owned R&D intensive companies to persuade them to carry out (more) R&D in the UK. It's an innovative initiative, using:

- R&D Specialists with detailed knowledge of technologies, and with commercial experience – able to get deep inside target company technology planning to establish what leading-edge R&D they want to develop and to set out the proposition for taking this forward in the UK.

- Virtual Teams with membership drawn as appropriate from UKTI staff overseas and in the UK, RDAs and Devolved Administrations, BERR and other Government Departments, Research Councils and the Technology Strategy Board.

To date 60 overseas companies are being targeted with nine project successes (a decision to invest in the UK in R&D) directly resulting from the R&D Programme's interventions reported so far. Their individual values range from £150,000 to £20 million. A further 11 project successes are expected by end March 2008.

cooperation frameworks, the UK-China Partners in Innovation and UK-Brazil Partners in Science initiatives. These bilateral mechanisms are being used to coordinate and underpin a wide range of UK initiatives.

6.20 One prominent cross-Government scheme aligned to the GSIF strategy is the UK India Education and Research Initiative (UKIERI), which aims to create a step change in educational and research links between the UK and India over a five year period.

6.21 An important element of meeting international development goals is to encourage research and innovation in developing countries – a factor which was recognised by the Commission for Africa as critical to accelerating their economic growth.[82] DIUS has supported follow up to the G8 African development agenda in a number of ways, including a dedicated science and education team within the Association of Commonwealth Universities to build better bilateral and multilateral links in this area and lead an FP7 consortium for sub-Saharan Africa, as an important contributor to the EU:Africa Strategic Partnership.

The Lisbon agenda

6.22 The Government has been influential in positioning research and innovation as core priorities of the revamped Lisbon growth and jobs agenda. This ambitious programme of work has included negotiation of important new spending programmes, notably the launch of new multi-billion euro technology development programmes (Joint Technology Initiatives) in areas of key UK strength (aerospace and pharmaceuticals) and the creation of a new European Institute for Innovation and Technology (EIT).

6.23 The UK has supported the establishment of Lisbon National Reform Plans, which are updated annually by all Member States and include a section on the progress made in the field of research and innovation in the context of the aim to raise overall EU investment in R&D to 3% of GDP. The UK has also been at the forefront of progress towards making the European Research Area (ERA) a reality, for example in developing a more strategic approach towards the establishment of new infrastructure facilities and mobility of researchers. The UK Presidency of 2005 was instrumental in securing agreement to a revamped Seventh Framework Programme (FP7), which provides considerable opportunities to the UK research community to collaborate internationally

6.24 It has proved difficult to make substantive progress in securing major improvements to the European patent system, though the recent ratification of the London Agreement will bring down the costs of translations. Government's aim is to achieve an affordable, fair and high-quality European patent court, which meets the needs of patent owners and users as a precursor to negotiating a single Community patent.

Implement the GSIF strategy and Sainsbury Review to promote the UK as a world class location to conduct innovation

6.25 In line with the recommendations of the GSIF Strategy and the Sainsbury Review, the Government will intervene selectively to improve the co-ordination of the UK effort overseas, to tackle barriers to effective cross-border collaboration and to better market the UK innovation offer.

## Capitalise on the creation of DIUS

6.26 In recognition of the importance of overseas science and innovation attachés to its international objectives, and those of GSIF partners, DIUS will assume responsibility for leading and managing the Science and Innovation Network (SIN). DIUS and FCO will co-fund this network in future and DIUS will host a management team of DIUS and FCO staff to oversee the network's operation

6.27 During the course of 2008 DIUS will produce an initial forward-looking international strategy, which will draw together inter-related policies within DIUS' remit, encompassing higher and further education, skills, research and innovation.

6.28 The Technology Strategy Board will advise Government on the opportunities which may arise from the adoption of EU regulations to stimulate business innovation including, where appropriate, building these into the design of Technology Strategy Board programmes. EU environmental regulations, such as those relating to water quality, have played a role in driving the growth of environmental industries, now a significant sector within the UK economy.

## Encourage UK business participation in EU programmes

6.29 In order to tackle the issue of relatively low participation by UK firms in European research programmes, the Technology Strategy Board will develop, as part of its international strategy, a marketing plan to help deliver a step change in the level of UK business participation in consortia competing successfully for grants in FP7. The Technology Strategy Board will implement this initiative in close cooperation with other delivery partners, notably the RDAs, DAs and Knowledge Transfer Networks (KTNs).

6.30 The Government will draw on the Technology Strategy Board's technical expertise and understanding of UK business strengths to help ensure that the periodic updating of FP work programmes achieves maximum coherence with the UK's national technology priorities.

DIUS will assume responsibility for leading and managing the FCO Science and Innovation Network (SIN). In the future, DIUS and FCO will co-fund this network and DIUS will host a management team of DIUS and FCO staff to oversee the network's operation.

During 2008 DIUS will produce an international strategy which will draw together inter-related policies within DIUS' remit, encompassing higher and further education, skills, research and innovation.

The Technology Strategy Board will develop, as part of its international strategy, a marketing plan to help deliver a step change in the ability of UK business to compete for grants in EU Framework Programme 7.

DIUS will work with BERR on implementing the European Commission's lead market initiative so that the UK's most innovative businesses can take advantage of the European single market and of new technology-driven global markets.

The Technology Strategy Board will advise Government on the opportunities which may arise from the adoption of EU regulations to stimulate business innovation including, where appropriate, building these into the design of Technology Strategy Board programmes.

6.32 The Government will continue to press the Commission to make the European research programmes as business-friendly as possible and welcomes several recent initiatives in this direction. Consequently, the UK will participate in two new "Article 169" joint Member State-Commission programmes, namely the "Eurostars" programme targeted at research-performing SMEs and Ambient Assisted Living (AAL) aimed at improving the quality of life of older people through the use of ICT. The Government will press the Commission to launch a similar initiative in the field of metrology, an area in which the UK excels and where the potential for benefits to accrue from greater European-level coordination is considerable. The Government will monitor actively the rollout of the Joint Technology Initiatives (JTIs) in 2008 and work

with European partners to facilitate the success of the set-up phase of the EIT scheduled to take place in 2009.

## Advocate EU budget reform

6.33 The Government regards refocusing the EU budget on addressing the challenges of globalisation as a priority. This implies more emphasis on research and innovation. If Europe is to reform its economy into the most dynamic and knowledge intensive in the world, then the resources and instruments at its disposal must be optimally deployed to serve this goal.

### Improve the European patents and wider international IP regimes

6.34 The Government continues to attach particular priority to improving the patent system in Europe, with the aim of fostering innovation. This means as a first step achieving an efficient, high-quality and affordable European patent court which meets the needs of patent owners and users and benefits all innovative companies. This must provide clear added value in relation to the existing system. Our ultimate goal remains agreement on a single Community patent. In the wider global context we will: seek to ensure that UK business knows how best to use overseas IP systems; make access to international IP simpler and less costly; increase the predictability of the effects of international IP systems; and ensure that all, especially developing countries can benefit from joining international IP regimes and thus expand a balanced and fair global market.

## Commitments

**UKIPO will seek progress in relation to a European Patent Court as a step towards the longer term goal of a single Community Patent.**

## Support Lead Markets in Europe

6.35 DIUS will work with the Department for Business, Enterprise and Regulatory Reform (BERR) on the action plans implementing the European Commission's lead market initiative[83] so that Europe's suppliers can grow to take advantage of the European single market and of new technology-driven global markets. Through more effective coordination between different policy areas, the aim is to identify and remove obstacles to private investment, particularly in markets (for example, renewable energies and ehealth) which directly impact on the attainment of public policy objectives and where public authorities play a key role in stimulating demand, whether as procurers, regulators or standard-setters. We will seek to ensure that the definition of the markets and is sufficiently broad to avoid the risks inherent in "picking winners".

# 7. Innovative People

*Most new ideas do not come as a flash of inspiration to a lone genius inventor, they come from how people create, combine and share their ideas. The UK's capacity to unlock and harness the talent, energy, and imagination of all individuals is crucial to making innovation stronger and more sustainable.*

*The effects of innovative people are self-reinforcing – innovative businesses are attracted to highly skilled and creative workforces and, in turn, innovative people are drawn towards exciting and challenging career opportunities. Furthermore, innovative people generate new ideas that require skilled people to implement and exploit them.*

*Government influences the UK's supply of innovative people through its funding of higher education, further education, Sector Skills Councils and National Skills Academies. To complement the previous focus on higher education, DIUS will establish a Further Education Specialisation and Innovation Fund, Sir James Dyson will establish the Dyson School for Design Innovation and, over the coming months, DIUS will consult on a Higher Level Skills Strategy and innovation will be an important element in developing a new 10 to 15 year*

*framework for higher education. These activities build upon the demand-led model of skills provision outlined by Lord Leitch.*

## The challenge

7.1 Innovation comes from how people create, share, refine and combine their ideas. Most new ideas do not come as a flash of inspiration to a lone genius inventor, they develop through collaboration and dialogue and through the application of a range of different skills from different parts of society. An economy's capacity to unlock and harness individuals' skills, talents, ideas and knowledge is crucial for innovation and wider economic and social benefits.

7.2 Innovation and skills are inextricably linked. A higher skilled and more expert workforce is more likely to be able to generate new ideas and to introduce and adapt to new technology and organisational change. In other words, skills are required for both the inventive part of innovation (where new technology, knowledge or processes are developed) and for the exploitation of those new inventions and knowledge. Evidence shows a clear relationship between the skill levels of the workforce and the extent to which firms are innovative[84]. As well as the scientific and technical skills that have long been associated with the development of new products, innovation today increasingly needs advanced management skills to adopt high performance working practices, creativity skills and a range of softer skills to support open innovation through co-operation with partners and supply chains.

7.3 In order to succeed Britain needs to make use of the talents of all our people and break down the barriers that prevent people realising their full potential. DIUS has a particular responsibility as the Department leading on science, innovation, skills, Further Education and Higher Education to ensure consistent and complementary policies across these areas.

## Where the UK stands

7.4 Government must ensure that people have the skills and knowledge necessary for innovation to occur. The Leitch Review of Skills, published in 2006[85], articulated the skills challenge we face. We have made real progress to improve our nation's skills in recent years. Over 1.75 million people have improved their functional literacy and numeracy skills since 2001. Around 100,000 apprentices now complete their apprenticeships each year in England compared to 40,000 in 2001/02. Participation in higher education amongst 18-30 year olds has grown from 39.3% in 1999/2000, to 42.8% in 2005/06. Despite this real and significant progress, Leitch concluded that to compete and prosper in the 21st century, we must commit to becoming a world leader on skills by 2020, benchmarked against the upper quartile of OECD countries.

7.5 Average management practices in UK firms often lag best practice: while good UK managers match the best in the world, there is a "long tail" of poor management in the UK which affects company performance,

particularly compared to the US[86]. It is estimated that differences in management practices between the USA and the UK account for 10 to 15% of the productivity gap between the two countries[87]. One consequence is that less skilled managers may place less emphasis on innovation and raising value-added than more skilled ones. This lack of strategic positioning, in turn, can affect the supply and demand of skills: in particular, managers do not demand higher skills as they are engaged in the provision of low specification products while workers have few incentives to obtain high skills given a lack of demand for such skills from managers.

7.6 *World Class Skills: implementing the Leitch Review of Skills in England*[88], published in July 2007, set out how Government will take forward the recommendations made by Lord Leitch and work with employers, individuals, partners and the Further and Higher Education sectors to ensure our nation's skills base is world-class by 2020. The progress we want to make towards that 2020 ambition by 2010-2011 is reflected in the Government's public service agreement for skills.

## How Government Can Support Innovation and What More It Will Do
### Further education

7.7 There are many examples of FE providers going beyond the provision of skills to deliver specialist research, consultancy and support for product development, process improvement, and business incubation.

7.8 In 2005, the Sector Skills Development Agency on behalf of the then Department for Education and Skills (DfES) and the Learning and Skills Council (LSC), produced the study *Talking the right language: can further education offer support for business innovation?*[89]. This

## St Helen's College

St Helen's College is an example of how working closely with local and national businesses and universities can encourage innovation. The college purchased an X-ray Florescence Spectrometer to provide an industry-standard item of equipment with which to attract trainees from local and regional SMEs. This has allowed St Helen's to improve links with regional businesses, raise their profile and host the first international X-ray Florescence Spectrometer workshop outside of the USA. St Helen's has also joined with Liverpool John Moores University in supporting the Merseyside Automotive and Manufacturing Group to develop capability and expertise in the sector.

showed that exchanges between SMEs and further education colleges benefit both parties. The Sainsbury review recognised the potential of the FE sector to encourage innovation, through links such as these.

7.9 As recommended in the Sainsbury review, DIUS has developed a strategy for promoting and supporting FE Knowledge and Technology Transfer (KTT) more widely within the FE reform agenda. The strategy will include:

• Workforce modernisation – including staff secondments to and 2-way exchanges with business, and increasing FE participation in Knowledge Transfer Partnerships.

• Promoting FE KTT to business – including further RDA investment in regional FE initiatives, working through Business Links to raise awareness of the FE offer to employers and promoting the FE offer to local Employment and Skills Boards through RDAs and Regional Skills Partnerships.

• Building capacity in FE KTT – including using National Skills Academies and wider Specialist Networks to replicate best FE KTT practice across the FE system, and recognising this capacity building effort as evidence for the continuous improvement aspects of new standard accreditation.

*What more the Government will do*

7.10 Government is keen to encourage individual FE providers to showcase their expertise in implementing innovative business solutions, particularly for SMEs. Above all, however, DIUS is keen to find ways to accelerate the building of knowledge and technology transfer capacity across the whole of the FE System, by "hot-housing" the expertise of the strongest providers. DIUS is confident that National Skills Academies and their specialist FE networks are the best way to focus effort on building the capacity of the FE workforce to be responsive, vocationally excellent and innovative.

7.11 In order to accelerate these reforms DIUS will allocate revenue funding for a number of pathfinder projects through an FE Specialisation and Innovation Fund. This will complement the £180m Specialisation and Innovation capital fund available from the LSC from 2008, earmarked for the development of National Skills Academies (NSAs) and investment in industry standard specialist facilities. It will also underpin the work of the Technology Strategy Board which is taking forward the Sainsbury recommendation to double the number of Knowledge Transfer Partnerships, increasing their flexibility and applicability to FE colleges and training providers.

7.12 A small number of pathfinder projects covering a range of networking arrangements, including FE providers networking with NSAs, Sector Skills Councils (SSC), Higher Education

Institutions, Regional Development Agencies (RDA), Regional Skills Partnerships (RSP), employers and supply chains will be set up.

7.13 Many of these network membership combinations already exist and DIUS is keen to better understand their variety and potential. DIUS believes that pathfinder projects are needed to point the way to how we accelerate capacity building in the skills, behaviours and business processes needed for successful knowledge and technology transfer. Government will particularly encourage two types of pathfinder projects:

• those where National Skills Academies (NSA) play a proactive role in leading the capacity building effort across their specialist networks, especially where there is already strong RDA and RSP engagement.

• those aimed at building capacity in the most challenging aspects of meeting the Training Quality Standard (TQS).

• Mechanisms for embedding this learning in other specialist networks, and growing the size and number of specialist networks, will be a key element of these projects.

7.14 The Learning and Skills Council's (LSC's) capital investment will continue to support specialisation within the FE sector, as part of the renewal and modernisation of the FE estate. The LSC will particularly welcome applications to the FE Specialisation and Innovation capital fund that support this activity.

7.15 Government is keen to promote the provider skills, behaviours and business processes that drive innovative business solutions, and believes that Training Quality Standard (TQS) accredited providers are the most likely to be able to signpost these. TQS is the new standard for employer responsiveness and vocational excellence. It has been designed by employers and SSCs and is proving popular with FE providers. Accredited providers have to demonstrate the responsiveness of their employer facing services. They can also apply for "centre of excellence" status. This is used by most NSAs as a requirement for membership of their specialist networks.

7.16 National Skills Academies offer a particularly innovative way to focus the efforts of the FE system on delivering the future-focused solutions that employers need. NSAs are proving popular with employers and there will be 12 in place by the end of 2008. There are already fully approved National Skill Academies in: Construction; Manufacturing; Financial Services; Food and Drink Manufacturing; Nuclear; and Process Industries. Six others are in business planning in: Hospitality; Creative and Cultural; Sport and Active Leisure; Retail; Glass Manufacture, Coatings, Print, and Building Products; and Fashion, Textiles, and Jewellery.

7.17 Demand for NSAs continues to rise strongly and it remains DIUS' ambition to have at least one NSA in every major sector of the economy, resources permitting. Bids are being actively encouraged from innovative industries such as Space, as well as cross-cutting bids from Healthcare Commissioning, the Environmental Industries and Enterprise, for example.

7.18 The Government is working with the well-known entrepreneur Peter Jones to develop plans for a National Enterprise Academy (NEA), as announced in BERR's Enterprise Strategy.[90] Government sees the NEA as having an important role to play in fostering innovation, by equipping people with the skills and talents to develop new ideas, create new products and services, and see them through.

# Innovative People

## Dyson School of Design Innovation

Alongside the National Skills Academy (NSA) programme, Sir James Dyson is working with the Government to launch the Dyson School of Design Innovation (DSDI). The main purpose of the new Design School will be to produce a new generation of engineers and designers who will help to secure a prosperous future for the UK.

James Dyson has noted that:

*"Creativity has an enormous part to play in design and engineering to address the big and exciting challenges ahead – environmental, demographic and ethical. But when we look at the numbers of young people actually studying design, technology and engineering, the situation is very worrying. We need to form the next generation of designers and engineers."*

The new School will be a National Centre of Excellence for design engineering offering new and exciting approaches to hands-on learning. Industry specialists from companies such as Airbus and Rolls-Royce as well as Dyson, will have a real involvement in the curriculum, giving students an understanding of the leading role UK engineering plays in the world economy. Using real, current and challenging problems from industry, students will be encouraged to create their own design solutions.

It is planning to open its doors to learners in September 2010. Working with local schools and colleges, National Skills Academies and universities, it will offer a range of provision for 13-19 year olds. It will also offer adult programmes, including Continual Professional Development for teachers, provision as the national centre of excellence, and degree and adult courses in Design and Engineering.

to successful realisation. That is the essence of entrepreneurship, which is an essential component of the Government's wider national strategy for innovation.

7.19 As part of the wider FE reform agenda Government is keen to modernise the FE workforce. A more specialised FE workforce will be better placed to propose innovative business solutions that have credibility with employers. The Lifelong Learning UK Catalyst programme gives further education staff the opportunity to update their specialist skills by working more closely with local businesses. BECTA, the Government's lead agency for Information and Communications Technology (ICT) in education, has developed a technology strategy which includes initiatives to develop the skills of the FE workforce to deploy technology effectively and efficiently. The Quality Improvement Agency is currently re-contracting for providers to deliver subject specific professional development for FE teachers and lecturers and encourage knowledge transfer with local industry.

7.20 The Learning and Skills Council's (LSC's) capital investment will continue to support specialisation within the FE sector as part of the renewal and modernisation of the FE estate. The LSC will particularly welcome capital applications that:

* support the specialist networks of new standard accredited providers growing up around the more progressive NSAs;

* give employers a role in developing or appraising proposals from providers to develop specialist skills infrastructure in their sectors; and

* enable specialist providers and specialist networks to deliver innovative business development solutions through technology and knowledge transfer.

7.21 Government also looks to Regional Development Agencies (RDAs) and Regional Skills Partnerships (RSPs) to encourage enterprise and business innovation. Government will look to encourage skills through regional investment in skills. There are Regional Skills Partnerships in each of the English regions which determine skills priorities and inform RDA investments. RDA funding is used to catalyse activity. With partners we will explore the potential for FE specialist networks to have a catalytic effect on businesses and on the skills system that align with regional priorities.

DIUS will drive implementation of the Leitch Review of Skills to raise the nation's skill levels and enhance opportunities for innovation, building implementation of the Sainsbury review recommendations into its wider strategies for FE reform.

DIUS will pilot a revenue-based FE Specialisation and Innovation Fund to build the capacity of the FE sector to support businesses to raise their innovation potential. Through a small number of targeted pathfinder projects DIUS will seek to unlock the talent of the FE workforce to drive business innovation through knowledge transfer.

Resources permitting, DIUS will aim to have at least one NSA in every major sector of the economy and is actively encouraging bids from innovative industries, including Space and the Environment.

Government is working with Peter Jones to develop plans for a National Enterprise Academy and with James Dyson to launch the Dyson School for Design Innovation

## Employers

7.22 As set out in *World Class Skills: Implementing the Leitch Review of Skills in England*[91], Government is committed to creating a demand-led skills system. Chapter 3 outlines plans for stimulating the demand for innovation; a skills system that responds to the needs of employers and employees is key to this.

7.23 Train to Gain is a core element of the Government's approach to delivering world-class skills. Through Train to Gain, employers can access support to help them identify and address their skills needs, including Government funding to sit alongside their own investment.

7.24 By December 2007, over 72,000 employers had engaged with Train to Gain, over a third of a million learners began learning programmes and almost 145,000 of these achieved their first full level 2 qualification. 74% of these employers were deemed "hard to reach" and 86% of employers say they are either satisfied" or "very satisfied" with the Train to Gain brokerage service.

### What more the Government will do

7.25 Over £1 billion a year will be channelled through Train to Gain by 2010-11. This is a doubling of the current Train to Gain budget and will ensure that more employers are able to address their skills needs and more employees can acquire new skills and unlock their talents. There are a number of specific ways in which Train to Gain will support the development of innovation skills:

• Programmes such as Business Improvement Techniques, which can introduce innovation in workplace practice.

- The Leadership and Management programme – over the next three years Government will increase annual investment in the programme, and from April 2008 eligibility will be extended to SMEs with between 10-250 employees (currently 20-250 employees). This £90 million investment will increase the skills of around 60,000 key directors and managers in approximately 42,000 SMEs.

7.26 The Government recently published *World Class Apprenticeships,* its strategy for apprenticeships in England. This sets out plans for a major expansion in the number of young people and older learners following this route. Evidence from many of Britain's leading employers suggests that the programme delivers important benefits to business, including a more self motivated, inquiring and productive workforce. For example, BAE Systems estimate that its apprentices are 50% less likely to make costly errors in the manufacturing and design process than non-apprentice trained recruits. They point to the highly developed problem solving abilities gained as part of their training programme as a significant factor in this. Other major companies such as BT, British Gas, Rolls Royce and Ford report similar outcomes.

7.27 Sector Skills Councils (SSCs) are key to making sure that the supply of skills and qualifications is driven by employer's needs, and helping raise employer ambition and investment in skills. DIUS is re-licensing SSCs: a central part of their revised core remit will be to ensure that they have a clear and authoritative picture of their current and future skills needs for their sectors. As part of that, SSCs will identify if there are particular skills gaps which need to be addressed to encourage further innovation in the sectors they represent, and consider how to promote innovation as a cross sector theme.

7.28 The establishment of the new UK Commission for Employment and Skills (UKCES) will create a powerful new employer voice at the centre of the skills system. The UKCES is interested in promoting productive deployment of skills across the UK, and innovation is an important element of wider productivity considerations.

7.29 However, innovation requires more than subject specific skills and knowledge. Leadership and management skills are vital in providing "space" for ideas, managing risk and being open to failure. Government supports the development of these skills through the Train to Gain Leadership and Management Programme. The UKCES will provide a further opportunity to support the development of these skills.

7.30 High Performance Working (HPW) is one area in which the UKCES can add particular value. High performance working recognises the importance of people management. The extent to which people's skills are utilised in the workplace affects organisational performance. For example, the focus is employee involvement and so effective job design is important to enable people to have enough responsibility and the means to express their views.

7.31 UKCES are looking to drive this forward in two areas:

- leading a major study of the nature, extent, and especially impact of HPW with a view to identifying the implications for policy and practice;

- working with partners to broaden knowledge of HPW practices and build management understanding and support for HPW across every sector.

**Government will continue to grow the Train to Gain programme and the Apprenticeship programme.**

**Reformed Sector Skills Councils will look to identify skills gaps which inhibit innovation.**

**The new UK Commission for Employment and Skills will pursue work on High Performance Working practices to increase value added in business.**

## Higher education

7.32 Since the Lambert Review in 2003, Higher education institutions have been increasingly positioned as agents for economic growth. Higher education institutions play a number of roles in innovation: research; teaching; exchanging knowledge; contributing to an international network of knowledge; and providing regional leadership. The Government is working towards a 10 to 15 year framework for the expansion and development of higher education. Innovation will be an important element of the strands (demographic changes, success criteria, student experience, intellectual property, relationship between academics and policymakers, international competitiveness, and widening participation) which have been commissioned to inform that framework. Universities are a focal point for people with the intelligence and imagination to develop solutions to global and domestic challenges and they can make the links between the development of innovative ideas and the teaching of skills to convert those ideas into commercial successes.

7.33 Universities provide the setting for people to acquire skills vital for innovation: specialist knowledge and higher-level skills; exposure to independent thinking, debate and creative problem solving; informal opportunities to learn through music, drama and third sector organisations. Universities attract talent and inward investment to a region; provide a bridge between public and private research; shape regional innovation strategies and stimulate social innovation though partnerships with local public and third sector organisations. They can stimulate and support enterprise and entrepreneurial activity.

7.34 The Government's New University Challenge underlines the importance of universities and Higher Education provision to the nation's economic and social success. The Government wants to accelerate the pace of development and expects to have 20 more opened or agreed over the next six years (in addition to the 17 that have been opened or committed since 2003), subject to high quality bids. These centres will widen participation and unlock talent and contribute to social cohesion. They will also help to drive economic regeneration and create a highly skilled workforce for the local business community as well as engaging with business to boost innovation.

## Case study

### Coventry University working with business

Coventry University is working with the AA, Caterpillar, Coventry and Warwickshire NHS Partnership Trust to develop the capability and competence of their middle managers to lead and innovate. In December 2006, The School of Lifelong Learning was awarded £3.5m by HEFCE to design and deliver a work-based development programme for managers in large organisations.

Designed with input from employers, the programme is customised in delivery to each individual organisation so that students use current, real time work challenges to stimulate and support learning. The resulting Capability Improvement Programme is a year long programme which supports participants to benchmark their current competence and extend their capability work. The programme also supports the development of organisational capability.

7.35 As well as research activities (Chapter 5), teaching at universities contributes to innovation. Higher education institutions have traditionally worked closely with professional bodies to deliver high-quality education that is relevant for the workplace. They also develop curricula and learning approaches, which help supply higher level, professional skills. However, there continues to be concern amongst employers that graduates lack employability skills.

7.36 Over recent years there has been a steady growth in the level of HEI-business interactions and funding streams have supported that trend. Since 2001, the Higher Education Innovation Fund (HEIF) has provided a third stream of HE funding in England and Wales to facilitate knowledge transfer from HE to business and the public and third sectors. Compared to research and knowledge transfer activities however, HEI-business interaction on workforce development is under-developed particularly in offering the flexible, work-based provision which employers demand. The HEFCE Strategic Development Fund has also given a boost to new policy directions such as workforce development and business engagement.

*What more the Government will do*

7.37 DIUS will shortly publish a Higher Level Skills Strategy. This will provide the overall framework for driving up the higher level skills that contribute to innovation in business. It will set out a clear aim – that Government wants both greater numbers of, and more employable, graduates and to raise the skills and capacity for innovation and enterprise of those already in the workforce. Achieving this is an economic imperative. There will be a consultation on the key proposals in the Strategy including how to further develop graduates' employability skills – particularly skills such as team working, problem solving, analytical skills, leadership and the ability to build and sustain relationships with colleagues and customers. Cognitive skills such as these tend to be the hallmark of successful innovators and are best learned young. The consultation will ask how we can help businesses and the higher education sector articulate, develop and deliver these skills more effectively.

7.38 At the same time the engagement of the higher education sector in workforce skills development must be strengthened markedly. This includes building on knowledge transfer activities to influence the development of professional and specialist skills in the workforce.

In consulting on the Higher Level Skills Strategy, Government will ask what more needs to be done to create the right conditions and incentives to stimulate and meet business, employer and student demand for higher level skills.

7.39 There has been a significant expansion of programmes supporting enterprise and entrepreneurialism in universities. These are linked to objectives around preparing students for employment, and working with business on knowledge transfer. DIUS will work with BERR and the National Council for Graduate Entrepreneurship to develop a new regional programme with the support of major businesses.

DIUS will shortly publish a Higher Level Skills Strategy. This will provide the overall framework for driving up the higher level skills that contribute to innovation in business.

The Government will develop a framework for the further expansion and development of Higher Education and has asked HEFCE to consult on how the 20 new HE centres can unlock human potential and drive regeneration.

DIUS will work with BERR and the National Council of Graduate Entrepreneurship to develop regionally-based University Enterprise Networks

## Science, Technology, Engineering and Mathematics (STEM) skills

7.40 The Government is committed to increasing the number of young people studying science, technology, engineering and maths at HEIs. There are encouraging signs that the Government's policy is starting to work. The most recent UCAS figures for 2007 university entry show increases in physics (up 10.3%), chemistry (up 8.3%) and maths (up 9.2%).

Engineering too has gone up by 4.3% overall.

7.41 DIUS plays a key role supporting STEM subjects, including additional commitments by HEFCE (£160m over 5 years), to increase the demand for and supply of students studying strategically important STEM subjects. Activities include STEMNET, and the science and engineering ambassadors (SEAs) scheme – there are now more than 18,000 ambassadors who have a significant impact in influencing young people to look at STEM and STEM careers in a positive light.

7.42 Evidence from the 2007 UK Innovation Survey with respect to the employment of graduates shows that higher level and STEM skills are associated with introducing innovations and conducting research and development. Enterprises that are innovation active have roughly twice the share of graduate employees when compared to those which do not innovate. Furthermore, the presence of science and engineering graduates is particularly strongly associated with being innovation active. This illustrates the importance of the Government's commitment to widening participation in higher education generally and STEM skills in particular, in encouraging innovation.

7.43 The Government's New University Challenge underlines the importance of universities and Higher Education provision to the nation's economic and social success. The Government wants to accelerate the pace of development and expects to have 20 more opened or agreed over the next six years, subject to high quality bids. These centres will widen participation and unlock talent and contribute to social cohesion. They will also help to drive economic regeneration, and create a highly skilled workforce for the local business community, as well as engaging with business to boost innovation. DIUS expects to have 20 more new HE centres opened or agreed over the next six years, subject to high quality bids.

*What more the Government will do*

7.44 DIUS will continue to work closely with DCSF to develop a coherent approach to increasing STEM skills. Current evidence relates mainly to the supply of STEM skills, with much less analysis on the demand from employers in private and public sectors. DIUS intends to develop a better understanding of the demand for STEM skills (including an in-depth understanding of the need for different STEM specialisms, and the level of skills needed) from different sectors of the economy and to understand how the labour market affects supply through its impact on choices made at all stages of education and employment.

7.45 DIUS will be leading a programme of analysis to develop a view on the UK's future needs for STEM skills working with DCSF, BERR and the Prime Minister's Strategy Unit (PMSU) and drawing on expert input provided by the Research Councils and business, and will develop new policies as needed to ensure the supply of STEM skills.

## Young People

7.46 The work of DCSF is contributing to the development of an enterprising and innovative mindset in young people. Much of this work goes under the heading of "enterprise education" and has developed rapidly in recent years as a strand of education in schools and colleges. £210 million is being spent to develop enterprise capability over the next three years. This builds on considerable earlier investment such as the establishment of a Schools' Enterprise Education Network through which the training of teachers in enterprise education has included a package focused on innovation.

7.47 The introduction of the 14-19 Diploma from September 2008 will allow more young

**DIUS will lead a cross- Government project on labour market needs for STEM skills and follow through any necessary policy changes.**

**DIUS, with DCSF, will work to increase the numbers studying STEM subjects at school level and Further and Higher Education.**

people to combine applied and academic learning, thinking with doing. All 17 of the new qualifications are being developed in close partnership with employers (both directly and through Sector Skills Councils) and HEIs to ensure that young people are equipped with the skills and knowledge they need, including enterprise and innovation skills, for personal and professional success in the modern world.

7.48 The new Diploma will foster enterprise and innovation in young people across its constituent components. For example, a learner studying for a Diploma in Engineering might take units on "Innovative Design and Enterprise" and "Exploring Engineering Innovation, Enterprise and Technological Advancements" as part of their core learning. Students taking an Advanced (Level 3) Diploma will undertake an Extended Project which is designed to develop and apply skills which demonstrate initiative and enterprise. The project might involve students engaging with a business or community venture/enterprise.

7.49 The Welfare Trust has created Project Enthuse which will provide a comprehensive funding and support package to enable all secondary schools to develop the skills of their science teachers at the National Science Learning Centre. The Government will invest £10 million over 5 years to support the scheme levering up to £20 million of investment from business and the Welfare Trust.

## Employees (%) educated to degree level by sector in innovation active and non-active firms[92]

### Innovation Active Firms

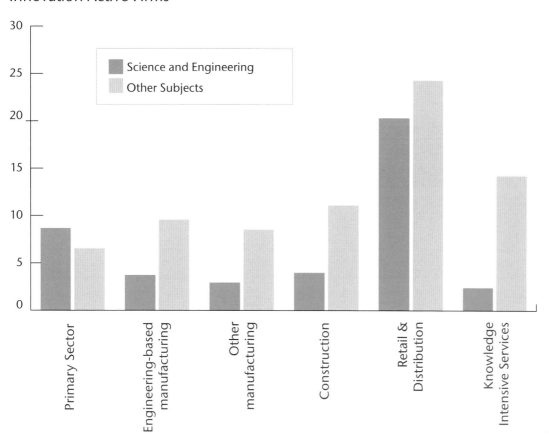

### Non-innovation Active Firms

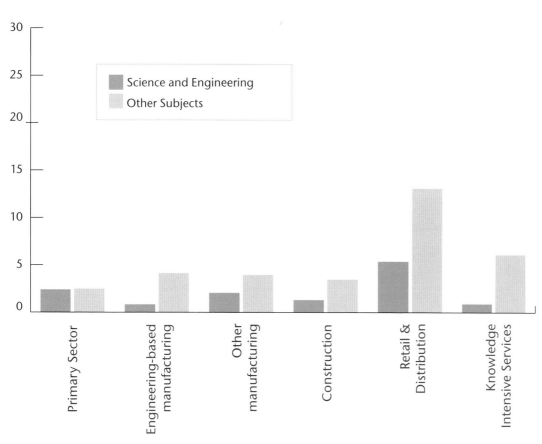

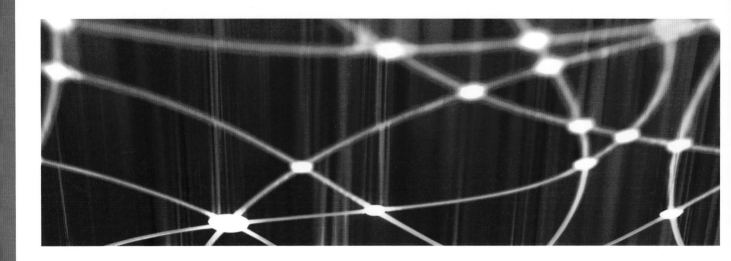

# 8. Public Sector Innovation

*Innovation in public services will be essential to the UK's ability to meet the economic and social challenges of the 21st century. Education, health and transport provide the underpinning for all innovative activity. Demand is growing amongst public service users for more efficient services that are personalised to their needs.*

*The Government can drive innovation in public services through the way it allocates resources and structures incentives. Major forces such as attitudes to risk, budgeting, audit, performance measurement and recruitment must be aligned to support innovation. Together and with effective leadership, these will progressively overcome existing cultural and incentive barriers. Those responsible for public service delivery must also learn the lessons of open innovation and adopt innovative solutions from the private and third sectors.*

*The NAO will conduct an audit-orientated study on innovation in the public sector. NESTA will establish a Public Services Innovation Laboratory to develop and trial the most radical and compelling innovations in public services. DIUS will establish a Whitehall Innovation Hub to disseminate learning from this and other sources to improve understanding of innovation at the highest levels of Government. DIUS will also convene a network of senior Whitehall innovators.*

## The Imperative for Innovation in Public Services

8.1 As outlined in the Prime Minister's Strategy Unit report *Realising Britain's Potential: Future Strategic Challenges for Britain* (February 2008), the defining social challenges of the 21st century – climate change, an ageing population and globalisation – will not be solved by "off-the-shelf" answers. Meeting them will depend increasingly on innovative solutions that raise standards, meet new objectives and improve efficiency.

8.2 The expectations of public service users are rising. Customers rightly expect an ever-higher quality of public services that are more personalised and responsive to their needs – from general practitioners open in the evening and at weekends and one-to-one tuition to personal budgets such as Skills Accounts that allow learners to control their own learning journey. Citizens have more information to compare public and private services and will set their expectations accordingly.

8.3 Successful innovation will require cultural and organisational change. Challenges do not respect traditional Departmental, service and sectoral boundaries and so new partnerships are necessary to generate and realise innovative approaches. There is an increasing recognition that the empowerment and incentivisation of front line workers and end users will be pivotal to achieving this.

8.4 The scale of service transformation mapped out in Sir David Varney's report *Service Transformation: A better service for citizens and businesses, a better deal for the taxpayer* (2006) will require innovation across the board:

• incremental innovation to improve existing services often by using new technologies to improve access and responsiveness;

• organisational innovation to create new joined up services, such as integrated children's centres;

• self directed services that will give users much greater control in shaping services to their needs; and

• long term systemic innovation to shift entire infrastructures of provision, for example in health care, towards promoting well being and healthy lifestyle management in the community.

## Where the UK Currently Stands

8.5 There is sometimes a perception that the public sector is out of touch with its consumer base, slow to respond to changes in the market place, bureaucratic, monolithic and inflexible, and a poor "second best" to the private sector in its ability to innovate. In fact, there is far more innovation in our public sector than people realise. Britain has a long track record of public services innovation, from the first public libraries, police, postal and fire services through to public parks, the creation of the BBC and the NHS[93].

8.6 Over the last few years a number of "intermediary bodies" have been established or developed to support innovation in public services. These range from units within or at arms length from Government departments (NESTA, NHS Institute for Innovation and Improvement) to organisations spun off from Government Departments (eg The Innovation Unit) to completely independent entities (eg The Young Foundation). In addition, many consultancies and think-tanks, commercial and non-commercial, provide assistance to local innovators.

8.7 The increasing involvement of the private and third sector in the delivery of public services is helping to maintain and stimulate innovation. The DeAnne Julius review of the public services industry will look into these and wider issues around the involvement of the private sector in supplying services across Government. This will complement research activity currently being undertaken by the Young Foundation, NESTA and others looking at the role of the third sector in driving innovation in public services[94].

8.8 Local Government and front line delivery bodies can be a rich source of innovations in the public services. *The National Improvement and Efficiency Strategy*, a joint central/local government publication issued in December 2007, states that increasing local government's innovative capacity to respond to future challenges is central to improved local performance. The Improvement and Development Agency for Local Government (IDeA) is leading the development of a new single integrated approach to support and review innovation at a local level.

## Case study

### Designs of the times (Dott)

As part of Dott 07, a programme of design innovation projects run by the Design Council and Regional Development Agency One NorthEast, a group of designers were asked to tackle the challenge of reducing domestic energy consumption. The design team set themselves the aim of reducing energy usage by 60% of one home in an economically deprived area.

The results of the project were a number of prototype services for local residents – all of which enabled them to cut their energy consumption and save money including:

- An "energy dashboard" (smart metering technology to provide real-time energy consumption to domestic users via their TVs, mobile phones or computers)

- NESCO – a not-for-profit energy utility that allows individual members of a local co-operative to buy a certain amount of energy at normal market rates, while benefiting from making energy savings via an incentive scheme

- SaverBox – a "pay-as-you-save" scheme which helps people pay for energy-efficient home improvements

8.9 A rigid focus on inputs and outputs rather than broad outcomes can create perverse incentives as public sector and service workers comply with the letter of the law rather than its spirit. For instance, it has been suggested that targets for an appointment to see a GP within 48 hours has seen some surgeries not accepting advance bookings[95].

8.10 More must be done to stimulate and support innovation in public services. The major forces that govern the public services (such as policy, budget requirements, guidance and legislation, and performance reporting) are not designed to create the incentives, signals and spaces for innovation and often create barriers and a heightened aversion to risk.

### How Government Can Support Innovation and What More It Will Do

8.11 Individual Departments have made significant strides over recent years to improve their ability to drive innovation.

8.12 In addition to initiatives and projects instigated by individual Departments, there are also significant achievements across Government through activities such as the HMT and Cabinet Office initiative Invest to Save, the Chief Information Officer's innovation work programme and the Transformational Government agenda. DIUS and OGC have also published guidance on procuring innovative solutions

8.13 However, until now these various initiatives have not been coordinated to form a cross-governmental programme to drive innovation in public services.

8.14 Whilst much progress has already been made, the Government is now committed to achieving a step-change in innovation performance that will require simultaneous work on five levels:

- creating the conditions for innovation by aligning the major forces of the public sector to be pro-innovation;

## Health Innovation Council and the NHS National Innovation Centre

Innovation is a key theme in Department of Health's future direction setting for the NHS. The NHS Next Stage Review will be setting out a 10 year vision. As part of this, the Department of Health has also established a Health Innovation Council chaired by Lord Darzai. In October 2007 the Council is to take a lead role in promoting and championing innovation from discovery through to adoption, holding the Department of Health and the NHS to account for taking up innovation and helping overcome barriers to doing so.

The NHS National Innovation Centre (NIC) was originally conceived by a cross-Governmental group as a catalyst for introducing innovations into healthcare. The NIC has devised an online toolkit and efficiently combines on-line and face-to-face contact to accelerate the development of technology based innovations into areas of need. With a focus on realistic solutions, the NIC commissions a rolling programme of 'Wouldn't it be great if...' (WIBGI) incubation projects within the NHS. The WIBGI Incubation projects enable healthcare professionals to work with designers, companies and other innovators to produce optimal solutions to problems. Through open and transparent commissioning processes, innovators can compare and win performance managed contracts to design and develop the most compelling ideas.

- leading for innovation by promoting awareness at the highest levels of the Civil Service of the importance of innovation and of the principal tools that help it flourish within the public sector;

- supporting and disseminating successful innovations that are already underway but go unnoticed;

- drawing on all sources of innovation by engaging users and front line workers and looking at innovation systems in the third sector, private sector, Devolved Administrations and public sectors in other countries;

- realising the potential of innovation as an enabling force in driving related policy initiatives and change programmes such as, the Transformational Government agenda and the work of the Sector Skills Council for Government (GovSkills).

8.15 The Government has set aside over £2.5 billion in the CSR to support and promote public service innovation over the next three years. This includes:

- £600 million in the Transport Innovation Fund which supports innovative proposals to improve transport in local areas;

- £164 million for the City Challenge fund for education, delivering innovative approaches to school improvement in challenging urban areas;

- £150 million in additional Continual Professional Development so every teacher is supported with training in the most innovative and effective professional practice;

- £1.2 billion for the National Police Improvement Agency which supports innovation and improvement across police forces;

- £27 million for the Social Enterprise Fund, to support the development of social enterprise to transform health and social care services;

# Public Sector Innovation

- £518 million Social Care Reform grant for Local Authorities to redesign and reshape their systems to deliver world class social care;

- £60 million in partnership with the Welcome Trust for the Health Innovation Council which will promote the discovery and adoption of innovation throughout the health sector.

Together this investment demonstrates the Government's commitment to driving improvement and innovation across the public sector and, alongside increasing resources for core services, should ensure that all citizens benefit from better public services in the coming years.

### National Audit Office (NAO) review of innovation and risk management

8.16 Building on a 2006 NAO report *Achieving innovation in central government organisations* and supporting the work of the Risk and Regulatory Advisory Council (RRAC), the NAO will commence a review of innovation and risk management in central government. The NAO will also consider the scope for a Spring 2009 conference on innovation and risk management, in collaboration with Government Departments.

In order to assist policymakers in understanding the acceptable levels of risk in pursuing innovative policies, the NAO will conduct a study that will explore the role of risk in stimulating or stifling innovation in the public sector.

### Whitehall Hub for Innovation

8.17 The Sunningdale Institute will work with partners to create a new Whitehall Hub for Innovation, a new partnership of organisations to capture and disseminate learning about public sector innovation. Operating across central government, but working closely with

the Public Services Innovation Laboratory (below), the Whitehall Hub for Innovation will:

- capture and disseminate knowledge and learning from other sectors and create links with similar public sector innovation initiatives in Devolved Administrations;

- make appropriate connections to related Government work such as that of the Risk & Regulation Advisory Council, the Better Regulation Executive, the BERR Review of the Public Services Industry and the Transformational Government agenda;

- package and disseminate learning from the front line (from Public Services Innovation Laboratory pilots and other initiatives) to inform Whitehall policy makers on the barriers, incentives and rewards to innovation by front line workers and users at a service level and how optimal conditions for innovation can be nurtured through improved system design; and

- build the capability of senior policy makers to design policies and public management levers that are pro-innovation.

The Sunningdale Institute will work with partners to create a Whitehall Hub for Innovation, a new partnership of organisations to capture and disseminate learning about public sector innovation.

### Public Services Innovation Laboratory

8.18 Drawing on expertise internationally and in the third and private sectors, NESTA will form the centre of an open and collaborative approach to developing the radical innovations that will transform public services – the Public Services Innovation Laboratory. Operating with a significant practical programme the Laboratory will:

- work as appropriate with partners such as the Young Foundation, Innovation Unit, IDeA, Design Council and Innovation Exchange to trial new methods for uncovering, stimulating, incubating and evaluating the most radical and compelling innovations in public services;

- act as a focal point for collecting and facilitating learning about innovations in public services trialled elsewhere. In particular, work with the International Social Innovation Exchange, OECD and others to promote an exchange of knowledge with international peers;

- package and disseminate lessons learned to promote adoption at service delivery level and improve the innovation system that enables pilots to roll out nationally;

- use this knowledge to develop curricula, tools and services for the public service practitioner audience;

- based on this practical experience communicate findings on critical success factors or barriers to innovation at a service delivery level to relevant policy makers and the Whitehall Hub for Innovation.

8.19 DIUS will support NESTA in building the relationships necessary to make the Laboratory a success, particularly across Whitehall.

NESTA will establish a Public Services Innovation Laboratory. Working as appropriate with partners such as the Young Foundation, The Innovation Unit, IDeA, Design Council and Innovation Exchange, the Laboratory will trial new methods for uncovering, stimulating, incubating and evaluating the most radical and compelling innovations in public services.

## Designing Demand for the public sector

8.20 Designing Demand is a Design Council programme which has been helping many hundreds of UK firms to use design as a strategic tool to support innovation. DIUS will ask the Design Council to develop and trial an innovation-enabling programme for practitioners in the public sector along the lines of the private sector model. The Design Council has explored possible delivery channels with the NHS and local government bodies.

The Design Council will develop and trial an innovation-enabling programme of designing demand for practitioners in the public sector, along the lines of the existing private sector model.

## Develop a network of leading Whitehall innovators

8.21 A network of senior Whitehall staff engaged with innovation in public services will be formed to demonstrate commitment at a senior level of Government, promote a more joined up approach to innovation across departments and make links with other Government initiatives on public service improvement. The Network will:

- act as an advisory group for the early stages of other proposals on public sector innovation;

- champion the public service innovation agenda within Government Departments; and

- advise on an appropriate framework for Departments to feed into the Annual Innovation Report.

## Explore extension of Power to Innovate

8.22 The Power to Innovate allows the Secretary of State for DCSF to suspend or modify legislation that may be holding back innovative approaches to raising standards on the front line. For instance, schools, colleges of further education and training providers, local authorities or Trusts (acting on behalf of Trust schools) may apply for a time-limited order to allow the testing of an innovative idea that has the potential to improve outcomes for pupils and students.

8.23 No assumptions are made about the kind of ideas that could be supported. Since introduction in 2002, the Power has been used in a diverse range of innovative projects – from testing 'virtual' governance, to allowing a group of schools to introduce a Transitional Sixth Form for those pupils unlikely to be in education, training or employment after completing year 11. Power to Innovate inquiries have also prompted changes to general legislation, for example enabling schools to offer HE foundation modules. DIUS will work with the Cabinet Office to consider extending the value of a Power to Innovate' across other delivery models to enable front line staff to explore new ways of delivering services.

DIUS will consider, with the Cabinet office, the value of an extended "power to innovate", enabling front line staff to explore new ways of delivering high quality services.

## Develop metrics for innovation in public services

8.24 Metrics for public sector innovation will be needed to inform the Annual Innovation Report. The Innovation Research Centre and Innovation Index (see Ch 6) will consider the most effective metrics to track innovation in public services.

# 9. Innovative Places

*Despite the spread of global communications, innovation still tends to cluster in particular locations, whether they be urban, rural, regional or national. Not all knowledge can be codified and innovators are helped by interaction that thrives on trust and proximity. Aside from helping the supply of knowledge, clusters mean that innovative organisations can be close to their market and thereby able to anticipate future demands.*

*In the UK, innovation performance varies considerably from place to place. This is somewhat dependent on sectoral specialisation and history. Traditionally, the UK's innovation policy has been concentrated on high-tech manufacturing. In the future, spatial innovation strategies must build on each region's distinctiveness. Moreover, because of the internationalisation of knowledge production, many UK regions will increasingly depend not on the creation of knowledge but on its absorption from elsewhere.*

*Innovation often does not obey artificial administrative boundaries. DIUS will work with RDAs and the Technology Strategy Board to build a balance between coordination and intelligent competition across the UK. New Partnerships for Innovation will drive innovation by bringing together public, private and third sector organisations to come up with innovative solutions to local and regional challenges.*

## Place and Geography in Innovation Policy

9.1 Innovation, and how a place can benefit from it, differs from place to place. As the production of new knowledge becomes globalised, different places in the UK will innovate in different ways. The drivers of innovation come together in places and can be urban, rural, regional, national and international in nature, often crossing administrative boundaries. Government, Devolved Administrations, RDAs, universities, local authorities and other public bodies influence the "innovation ecosystems" in which they operate.

9.2 The challenge for policy-makers is to create a framework, at a national and sub-national level[96], where activities to support innovation are focused on co-operation between the different actors involved, are responsive to different places and spatial levels and work across administrative boundaries. This includes policies at a national or pan-regional scale and at a regional or sub-regional scale. The RDAs are well placed to lead this and to strengthen the innovation infrastructure within the English regions (for example reducing barriers to collaboration and improving access to "knowledge economy" assets). This strategy focuses on the ways in which Government and these actors develop and implement innovation policies appropriate to different places by setting.

## Where the UK Stands

9.3 While there are good data at a sub-national level of some of the indicators of economic and social prosperity, there are at present few equivalent data on innovation and this makes analysis of innovation performance difficult (see chapter 5 on proposals to tackle this). Survey-based measures of overall business innovation activity show relatively little variation across regions and countries within the UK.

**Innovation activity by region, 2004-06 %**

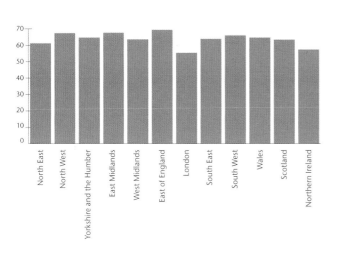

9.4 However more detailed innovation patterns do differ across regions and countries because of differences in the capacity of businesses to use and exploit knowledge; this is partly explained by the variation in sector distribution between regions. For example, R&D expenditure is concentrated in the south of England.

**Regional R&D expenditure by type, % of GVA, 2003**

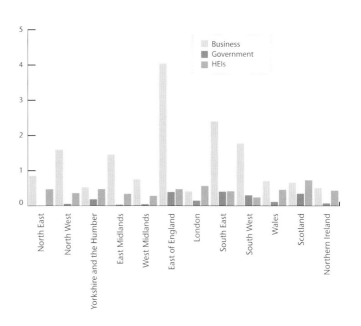

9.5 There are also differences in the numbers of skilled people, especially graduates.

**Highest qualification of economically active adults by region, 2006 Q4**

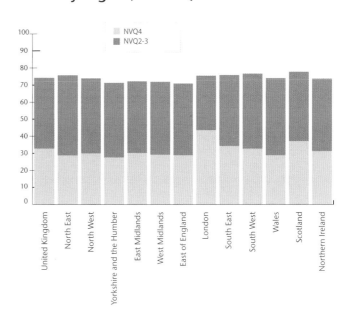

9.6 There is a growing body of evidence recognising the importance of cities and city-regions to the regional and UK economy and emerging research on rural innovation particularly as developed by organisations including NESTA, The Work Foundation and Centre for Cities.

## How Government Can Support Innovation and What More It Will Do

### Strategies for innovation

9.7 Regional Development Agencies, through their analytical work supported by the development of regional strategies, provide the strategic framework for economic growth and regeneration in their regions. Science and innovation plays a prominent role in these. RDAs work with a diverse range of stakeholders and their Science and Industry Councils to translate national policy into solutions that address regional priorities. As above, there needs to be a better understanding of the differences within regions.

- DIUS will work with RDAs, BERR and CLG to achieve a better understanding of the different patterns of innovation and ensure that action on innovation is taken at an appropriate spatial level and scale to ensure that innovation is recognised as a key element of the new integrated regional strategies.

- NESTA will, as part of its work to develop an Innovation Index, work with RDAs and DAs and the Innovation Research Centre to explore the scope for regional or sub-national innovation measures that capture spatial innovation patterns.

- DIUS will work with BERR, CLG and RDAs to ensure that Local Authorities consider the role that innovation plays in their local economy as part of their local economic assessments.

9.8 RDAs have collectively increased their spending on science and innovation, including support for business innovation and strengthening programmes of activity for partnerships. RDAs are key partners in the Business Support Simplification Programme and will ensure that alongside a consistent national support offering, there is also flexibility within regions to reflect the differing geographical spread and concentration of people, businesses, sectors and institutions.

9.9 RDAs support business innovation in a number of ways:

- supporting commercialisation – RDAs provide investment and help to businesses to develop routes to market as well as a coherent set of finance support measures to help a business at different stages of development;

- providing guidance on innovation – through the Business Links and investment in programmes providing subsidised access to an expert – for example, the Designing Demand Programme;

- knowledge exchange – for example through investment in facilities to help contact between academics and businesses;

- supporting networks of businesses, universities, research organisations and local Government; and

- identifying, with national and sub-national skills organisations, the supply and demand for skills within a region and the priorities flowing from that analysis.

9.10 DIUS will continue to work with RDAs and BERR to ensure that national frameworks are consistent with these mechanisms of support.

### Collaboration with the Technology Strategy Board

9.11 RDAs and DAs will work with the Technology Strategy Board in developing strategies and programmes for translational research, infrastructure and demonstration together with Research Councils. The publication of the Technology Strategy Board's technology strategy will provide further opportunities for collaboration, for example on Innovation Platforms and challenge based programmes.

9.12 RDAs and the Technology Strategy Board have put in place new arrangements to align their funding and activities to implement the recommendation in the Sainsbury Review to enable a collective RDA network investment of at least £180 million over three years (2008-11) in activities to support the Technology Strategy. The Devolved Administrations are also key partners in this collaboration and will align activity and resources where appropriate opportunities emerge.

9.13 DIUS will work with the various partners to ensure the effectiveness of these arrangements in delivering the Sainsbury Review recommendation. Progress towards achieving the £180m aligned funding will be tracked in the Annual Innovation Report.

Collaboration across and within regions
9.14 DIUS is a delivery partner with other Government Departments in delivering the Regional Economic Performance Public Service Agreement to improve the economic performance of all English regions and reduce the gap in economic growth rates between regions. The focus for Government activity in

**Collaboration between Technology Strategy Board, RDAs and DAs**

The Technology Strategy Board, RDAs and DAs have developed mechanisms for joint working to:

• improve strategic planning, communication and feedback between the Technology Strategy Board, RDAs and DAs and ensure that regional strategies reflect the national strategy and priorities and that national policy reflects and takes account of regional strengths and economic strategies;

• secure effective engagement and coherence between the Technology Strategy Board, RDA and DA planning, delivery and monitoring arrangements and streamline systems on both sides to make it easier and more attractive for RDAs/DAs to co-invest in Technology Strategy Board programmes and activities;

• achieve the CSR RDA commitment requiring RDAs to align £180m in 2008-11.

A Strategic Advisory Group has been established, chaired by the Chief Executive of the Technology Strategy Board, and comprising of Chairs or senior figures from each of the Science and Industry Councils (or Devolved Administration equivalent), together with representatives from other partner organisations. It will focus on shared strategic and long-term issues and take a strategic overview of Technology Strategy Board/regional collaboration.

An Operational Advisory Group comprises key operational staff in the Technology Strategy Board, the RDAs and DAs. The focus of this Group is agreeing, putting in place and overseeing mechanisms and processes, including regional prospectuses, to align Technology Strategy Board/RDA funding and delivery and to ensure an effective two-way channel of communication between Technology Strategy Board, RDAs and DAs.

delivering the innovation dimension to this PSA is in the North and a key partner is the Northern Way comprising the three Northern RDAs – One NorthEast, Yorkshire Forward and the North West Development Agency. DIUS will continue to support the Northern Way in developing and implementing its innovation strategy.

9.15 DIUS is working with all the RDAs to increase the innovation capacity of towns, cities and regions recognising that the regional innovation agenda has matured over recent years to move beyond high level common priorities across regions (eg many regions have biotechnology ambitions) to focus on the particular strengths within a region that the RDA and its partners support and develop.

9.16 RDAs are increasingly collaborating where there are shared reasons for doing so and competitive advantage can be increased. Government encourages such partnerships where increased benefit can be achieved. The three South Eastern regions have developed effective mechanisms for joint working as the Greater South East.

## The Northern Way

The Northern Way brings together the three regions of the North of England to cooperate in improving the economic development of the North towards the level of more prosperous regions. Led by the three northern RDAs, it has highlighted business innovation as a pan-regional priority across the North, particularly within high value added sectors where the North can potentially attain significant competitive advantage.

Since its formation in 2004, the Northern Way has added value by supporting cross-regional innovation capacity – for example in establishing both the Centre of Excellence for Biocatalysis, Biotransformations and Biocatalytic Manufacture (CoEBio3) and the Manchester Cancer Research Centre and by developing the North's creative and digital sector. The Northern Way has also supported the N8 partnership of Northern research-intensive universities to strengthen research capabilities and university-industry collaboration. The N8 has created five Research Centres involving 190 companies in fields where the North has critical mass of international expertise to tackle economic and social challenges: energy, sustainable water use, regenerative medicine, ageing and health, and molecular engineering.

The Northern Way is bringing together the three Science and Industry Councils with business and universities, to identify transformational initiatives to support new analysis and a stronger voice for the North in national policy development.

## Greater South East

The Greater South East, across three regional development agencies, is a polycentric network of small cities and towns surrounding London. Knowledge transfer is pan-regional and EEDA, LDA and SEEDA are developing joint innovation programmes to build on this strong connectivity and critical mass of creative human capital to increase the UK's global competitiveness.

A joint university business fellows and technology transfer programme, operated by the London Technology Network, is increasing business-university collaboration across the GSE. A joint innovation map and research excellence directory identifies the major strengths of each university and research establishment to promote the GSE as an international knowledge centre. Joint business support and knowledge networks that will enhance common strengths, are being developed, for example in security.

Innovation and skills will create business opportunities and drive market-oriented solutions to climate change and global warming. The three RDAs are working with businesses and universities and the Department of Communities and Local Government to help create the world's first major eco-region in the Thames Gateway which will create and access best international knowledge through the Institute for Sustainability.

## Science Cities

9.17 The Science City Programme shows how science and innovation partnerships can work well across institutions. Science City is a designation given by Government (building in some cases on existing partnerships) to six English cities: Manchester, Newcastle and York (designated in 2004); and Birmingham, Bristol and Nottingham (designated in 2005).

9.18 The Science City designation has successfully raised the profile of science and innovation within these cities and their respective regions. They have each established consortia involving RDAs, local authorities, universities and business to translate the designation into practical outcomes bringing together public and private investment in a range of policy areas including science, innovation, urban regeneration, education and business support.

## Case study

### Birmingham Science City

Science and technology are vital to the future development of the West Midlands region and Birmingham Science City is undertaking exciting work to create and use new knowledge for economic growth and improvements in quality of life.

Birmingham Science City is building on the outstanding knowledge and capabilities of the region's universities, developing strong relationships between industry. HEIs across the region are growing a diverse industry base, building on research strengths, which in turn will support the attraction of the region as a place to develop new businesses and, in conjunction with new innovative approaches to the challenge, increase the retention of graduates in the region.

The Birmingham Science City partners are delivering a number of demonstrator focussed projects. These act as exemplars to stimulate broader collaboration and knowledge transfer between knowledge base institutions and industry. These include a collaborative research and knowledge transfer programme between the Universities of Birmingham and Warwick, funded by the Regional Development Agency – Advantage West Midlands (AWM) – focussed on advanced materials, translational medicine and energy. The first major project is the Hydrogen Energy Project, where AWM's investment of £6.2 million is part of a 10 year project that is already attracting investment from public and private partners. An example of a shorter term project is the Ocular Allergy Project (run by Aston and Worcester Universities) which is investigating how allergies affect the eye.

9.19 The Science Cities designation also helped build understanding of the role of science and innovation as a strong promotional tool and developed capacity to innovate within regions through their partnership approach.

9.20 Beyond the Science Cities, RDAs are leading partnerships in regions to identify and catalyse activity to address innovation. Increasingly regional strategies are focusing on regeneration and economic growth driven by science and innovation e.g. Diamonds for Investment and Growth in the South East and Innovation Connectors in the North East.

9.21 Universities are key elements of local and regional innovation systems and contribute significantly to the innovative success of a place through regeneration and innovation activities. HEIs stimulate enterprise and entrepreneurship as well as supplying higher-level skills and supporting innovation. The innovation needs of business and the economic and social needs vary depending on the place and HEIs respond in different ways, ranging from high value-added knowledge intensive activity to more focused direct support for local businesses. The new 'University Challenge' will bring the benefits of local higher education provision to more parts of the country.

### New Partnerships for Innovation

9.22 DIUS recognises the progress that Science Cities have made in developing partnerships across a range of organisations, public authorities and businesses to achieve

## Case study

### Process industries in Tees Valley

The Centre for Process Innovation (CPI) has made a central contribution to the renewed growth and major new investment in the process industries in Tees Valley in North East England, leveraging £171m in investment in R&D and related innovation projects over the last three years. These industries, which are vitally important for the economy of the Tees Valley City Region and the North East as a whole, were facing an uncertain future as key industrial facilities and infrastructure declined.

CPI was formed in 2003 as a partnership of businesses, universities and the RDA, One NorthEast, to develop new innovations required for sustainable success. CPI worked with businesses across the world to identify their innovation needs and coordinated development programmes to meet these. It has established major shared assets such as the National Industrial Biotechnology Facility. The region has now seen significant new investment in innovative activities including R&D by international businesses, attracted in large part by this new capability.

The Wilton Centre is now one of Europe's largest technological innovation locations. In turn, this new investment and growth is revitalising the economy and employment prospects of its City Region.

shared innovation priorities and will champion their successes across Government. DIUS will build on their success by establishing New Partnerships for Innovation which will seek to bring together public, private and third sector organisations to develop innovative solutions to local and regional challenges, such as economic, social, environmental or a combination of these.

9.23 DIUS will consult with interested parties and publish a prospectus for the New Partnerships for Innovation in the Autumn. We expect them to involve local authorities, business, RDAs and further and higher education institutions. A key challenge for New Partnerships for Innovation will be to show how they will build links between the public finance available from innovation investments and private finance, including Venture Capital Trusts and Enterprise Capital Trusts.

9.24 These partnerships will not place new duties on or duplicate existing partnership arrangements. They will enable new innovation partnerships to develop around communities of interest with a strong sense of place large enough to have critical mass. Examples could include authorities and universities to provide a collective focus on innovation in key business sectors.

9.25 Other opportunities for partnership exist in the field of health. As part of the NHS Next Stage Review, the DH and DIUS will work together to ensure that research, teaching and clinical practice at all levels can be brought together across health and social care systems to further energise innovation in health delivery.

9.26 DIUS will work with RDAs, local authorities and their partners including business and universities to use Multi-Area Agreements (MAAs) where appropriate to promote innovation across the administrative boundaries of local authorities and approach innovation at an appropriate scale to be both efficient and effective.

9.27 Promoting a more entrepreneurial approach among university students is a practical step which can strengthen the innovative capability of a region. BERR and DIUS have therefore agreed to support the National Council for Graduate Entrepreneurship in setting up a new regional programme with the support of major businesses, including Microsoft UK.

9.28 The Design Council's Dott programme aims to improve public services through the application of design and user-focused innovation. Dott 07 was hosted by One NorthEast and involved more than 200,000 local people. DIUS will also support the Design Council in building the partnerships necessary to make the next phase of the Dott programme a similar success. Expressions of interest have already been invited from all regions for DOTT 2010 and advanced discussions are underway in both Scotland and Cornwall (through Cornwall County Council and SWRDA). Discussions are underway with the Technology Strategy Board to align Dott with some of the Innovation Platform themes including Low Impact Buildings and Assisted Living.

DIUS will sponsor New Partnerships for Innovation that will bring together venture capital, universities, business and regional government to align efforts and develop innovative solutions to local and regional challenges. DIUS will publish a prospectus for New Partnerships in Autumn 2008.

The Technology Strategy Board and RDAs will work to align their strategies and funding for technological research, demonstrators and Innovation Platforms and achieve the £180m aligned funding commitment.

As part of its work to develop an Innovation Index, NESTA will work with RDAs and DAs and the Innovation Research Centre to explore the scope for regional or sub-national innovation measures that capture spatial innovation patterns.

DIUS and BERR will build on the success of the National Council for Graduate Entrepreneurship by establishing a regional network which DIUS will co-fund.

DIUS will work with RDAs, the Technology Strategy Board, the Devolved Administrations, local authorities and other partners including business and universities to align national and regional innovation programmes and, where appropriate, to use multi area agreements to promote innovation across the administrative boundaries of local authorities.

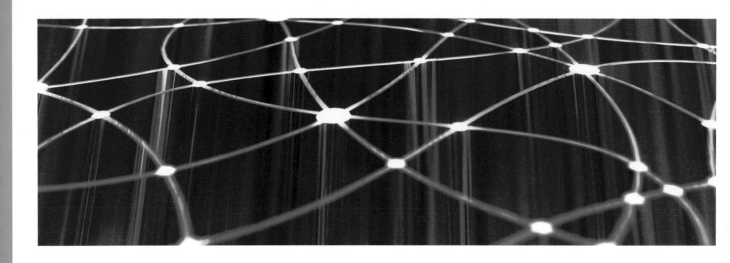

# 10. Innovation Nation: Next Steps

10.1 Government has the bold ambition of making Britain the leading place in the world in which to be an innovative business, public service or third sector organisation. This document has described what we need to do if we are to achieve this, and some of the milestones along the route. We have many strengths to build on, such as our excellence in scientific research, world-leading companies, bright, creative people and a diverse and vibrant innovation ecosystem. But there are areas we need to improve.

10.2 By bringing together in DIUS responsibility for science and the research base, innovation, universities and skills development, we have an opportunity to achieve a consistent and coherent approach to supporting innovation in the UK. This will help to create the Innovation Nation for the UK and its people to prosper in the 21st Century.

10.3 As well as setting this vision, we will need to demonstrate that we are delivering it. For this reason, the Sainsbury Review recommended that the Government should publish an Annual Innovation Report. This will enable all our stakeholders in business, in the public sector and in the third sector to see the progress that the Government, and particularly DIUS, have made in delivering the objectives of this Strategy and other policy documents. It will build on the first report on the implementation of the Sainsbury recommendations, which is published alongside this Strategy.

10.4 The first Annual Innovation Report will be published in Autumn 2008. It will be the first comprehensive report on the innovation performance of the UK across both public and private sectors. It will include an assessment (including an independent view) of the effectiveness of Government departments in supporting innovation through sponsoring research and development, support for the science base, use of procurement to drive innovation and the use of regulation and deregulation. It will also assess how Departments are improving their own innovative capability and that of the public bodies they sponsor.

10.5 The Annual Innovation Report will consider the performance of the wider public sector in supporting innovation including the RDAs, economic regulators, research councils and the HE and FE sectors. It will also report on the level of investment in R&D and innovation by UK business, and place this in the context of long term trends. It will highlight strengths and weaknesses, and key sectors or technologies where the UK needs to improve performance. The Report will also benchmark UK performance against that of key competitors, drawing on existing and new indicators, which will be developed to fill gaps in our existing knowledge.

10.6 NESTA will develop a new Innovation Index to measure UK innovation drawing on input and expertise from partners such as the ONS, DIUS, BERR, TSB, AIM, the Design Council, CBI and others. A pilot index will be published in 2009 with a fuller system in place by 2010.

10.7 The creation of an Index will enable NESTA to:

• identify gaps in current measures;

• embed existing innovation measures in a broader portfolio of other indicators that better reflect innovation outcomes and activities across the economy;

• improve our understanding of service sector, user-led and public sector innovation; and

• build on measures that innovative firms and their investors find useful.

10.8 DIUS, NESTA, ESRC and the Technology Strategy Board will create an Innovation Research Centre to ensure a steady supply of high quality innovation research into the UK innovation policy community.

# Annex: Development of this White Paper

Structured discussions were undertaken to identify discuss key issues concerning innovation in the UK and to solicit fresh ideas from a wide range of stakeholders. This was undertaken in the spirit of open innovation and has taken and responded to as wide an input as possible in the time available

The consultation consisted of two elements: a series of workshops between December 2007 and February 2008 involving face to face discussions and an open consultation through the web.

## Workshops

The workshop series were designed to:

• seek ideas from informed commentators across a range of sectors

• engage key stakeholders

• explore policy proposals with the community

Specifically, workshops were held on the following themes:

• definitions and measurement of innovation;

• public sector innovation;

• innovative people;

• business innovation;

• international innovation;

• innovative places;

• intellectual property;

• future of research;

• innovative users and consumers

Each workshop involved around 20 stakeholders from business, research, think tanks, education and public services. Ian Pearson, Minister of State for Science and Innovation, chaired the workshops.

Notes summarising key discussion points from each of the workshops are available at http://dius.dialoguebydesign.net/bgo/innovation%20news.asp

## Written Responses

Responses from 283 people and organisations were received from as diverse as a group of young people facilitated by the Learning and Skills Network to the National Consumer Council and from Pfizer to Papworth Hospital. The quality of responses was high and many of the policy themes and ideas put forward have been reflected in the Strategy.

The breakdown of source of responses is given below. The majority were either from businesses or organisations representing businesses.

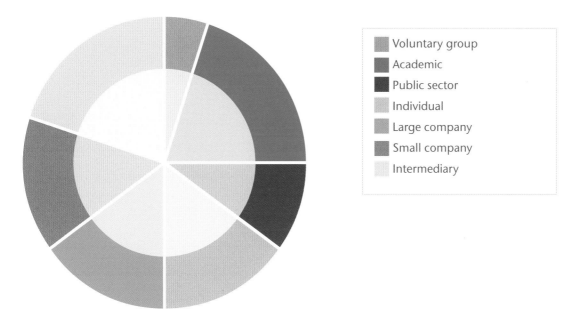

Voluntary group
Academic
Public sector
Individual
Large company
Small company
Intermediary

## Key Themes

It was clear that all responders believed that innovation was key to prosperity. There was also a high degree of consensus around a number of themes which were seen to be important.

• Procurement – There was consensus that Government should act as a lead user of innovation demonstrating new technologies and providing innovative solutions to public services and societal challenges. The substantial power of Government procurement should be brought to bear through "smart" procurement acting both as stimulus to innovation and giving the public long term value for money. A number of specific suggestions were given on mechanisms to achieve this and incentives.

• University Assessment – There was significant comment on the degree to which academics are incentivised to work with business through the HE funding system. It was considered that there was a bias towards

curiosity driven research recognised through academic paper production. The consensus was that researchers should be more rewarded for engaging with users on the full scale of activities through basic research to more applied demonstrator type activities.

• Widening the support for innovation to be broader in scope than science alone.

• There was widespread recognition that innovation is much more than technology with service and management innovation and incremental small step improvements being seen as key to effective innovation systems.

• Innovation vouchers – Many respondents supported the introduction of a national scheme for innovation vouchers particularly as a low cost taster for companies new to collaboration on innovation. Specifically it was noted that this approach put companies in the driving seat in engaging with the knowledge base.

- SET and Language skills – There was particular concern both over the quality and quantity of SET skills which it was perceived are the life blood of future innovation performance. Of particular concern was the skills mobilisation in the Far East and the relative competitive position of the UK. Skills were also seen as key in attracting high value added inward investment. The good work done to date was recognised but the need for on-going action recognised. Language skills were also seen as key in an increasingly global market place.

- Risk/innovation culture – There was consensus around the negative attitudes to risk in the UK highlighting the unacceptability of failure within UK society. This was particularly believed to be the case within the public sector which was seen as particularly risk adverse with an overly conservative view taking of the use of tax payers' money.

- Thinking skills in schools – Underpinning the ability of the UK to innovate is the ability for individuals to think creatively and develop problem solving skills. These are seen to be key elements requiring inspirational teaching throughout the school system.

- Public understanding and acceptance of science and technology – The public acceptance of science and technology was seen as key to opening up new markets and user acceptance of new technologies. Examples were given of where this had negatively effected the UK competitive position.

# Footnotes

1 Science policy applies UK wide; education and skills policies apply to England and Wales; some enterprise and innovation policies apply UK wide (eg the activities of UKTI and UK-IPO) and others apply to England only.

2 DIUS (2008) Background analysis: strengths and weaknesses of the UK innovation system

3 DTI (1998) *Our Competitive Future: Building the Knowledge Driven Economy*

4 DTI (2003) *Innovation Report*

5 HM Treasury (2004) *Science and Innovation Investment Framework* 2004 – 2014

6 Lord Sainsbury of Turville (2007) *The Race to the Top – A Review of Government's Science and Innovation Policies*

7 DTI (2007) *Implementing "The Race to the Top": Lord Sainsbury's Review of Government's Science and Innovation Policies*

8 This includes a series of workshops led by Ian Pearson MP, Science and Innovation Minister, as well as 283 written submissions, including online submissions (see Annex for more details).

9 NESTA (2006) *The Innovation Gap: Why policy needs to reflect the reality of innovation in the UK*. London: NESTA

10 DCMS (2008) *Creative Britain: New Talents for the New Economy*

11 HM Treasury (2005) *Cox Review of Creativity in Business: building on the UK's strengths*

12 DTI (2005) *Creativity, Design and Business Performance*

13 Andari, R., Bakhshi, H., Hutton, W., O'Keeffe, A. and Schneider, P. (2007) 'Staying Ahead: The economic performance of the UK's Creative Industries.' London: The Work Foundation.

14 Bakhshi H., McVittie E. and Simmie J. (2008) *Creating Innovation: Do the creative industries support innovation in the wider economy?* London: NESTA

15 Higgs P., Cunningham S. and Bakhshi H. (2008) *Beyond the creative industries: Mapping the creative economy in the United Kingdom*

16 NESTA (2007), *Hidden Innovation: How innovation happens in six 'low innovation' areas*. London: NESTA.

17 Dodgson G. and Gann D. (2007) *Innovation Technology: How new technologies are changing the way we innovate*. London: NESTA.

18 Waurzyniak P. (2007) 'Enter the Virtual World' *Manufacturing Engineering*. October 2007.

19 Chesbrough H. (2003) *Open Innovation: The New Imperative for Creating and Profiting from Technology*. Massachusetts: Harvard Business School Press.

20 Dyer J.H. & Hatch N.W. (2004) *Harvard Business Online* Vol. 45 (Reprint 45311 No. 3), pp. 57–63.

21 Huston L. & Sakkab N. (2006). 'Connect and Develop: Inside Procter & Gamble's New Model for Innovation'. *Harvard Business Review*. Vol. 84 (No. 3).

22 One paper, for instance, found that 82% of all functionally-novel products in the scientific instruments market were the result of user innovations. Riggs W. & Von Hippel E. (1994) 'Incentives to Innovate and the Sources of Innovation: The Case of Scientific Instruments'. *Research Policy*. Vol. 23 (no. 4), pp. 459–469. It should be noted, however, that encouraging user-led innovation has long been a conscious strategy in the scientific instruments business. For further examples, see Von Hippel, E. (2002) 'Horizontal innovation networks – by and for users.' MIT Sloan School of Management Working Paper No. 4366-02.

23 Von Hippel, E. (2005) *Democratizing Innovation* Massachusetts: MIT Press.

24 Chatterji A. K. and Fabrizio K. (2007) 'Professional Users as a Source of Innovation: The Role of Physician Innovation in the Medical Device Industry' *Berkeley Working Paper*. Riggs W. and Von Hippel E. (1994) 'Incentives to Innovate and the Sources of Innovation: The Case of Scientific Instruments,' *Research Policy*. Vol. 23 (no. 4), pp. 459–469.

25 This is also broadly consistent with the spirit of Aghion P., Dewatripont M. and Stein J. C. (2005) 'Academic Freedom, Private-Sector Focus, and the Process of Innovation,' Harvard Institute of Economic Research Discussion Paper No. 2089, in which the authors discuss the exploratory advantages of academic freedom.

26 OECD (2006) 'OECD Science, Technology and Industry (STI) Outlook 2006.' Paris: OECD

27 UNESCO (2006) 'Global Education Digest 2006 – Comparing education statistics across the world.' Montreal: UNESCO Institute for Statistics.

28 OECD (2007), *Globalisation and Regional Economies: Can OECD Regions Compete in Global Industries?* OECD Reviews of Regional Innovation

29 Demos (2008) *Atlas of Ideas II*, forthcoming.

30 Georghiou L. (2007) *Demanding Innovation: Lead markets, public procurement and innovation*, London: NESTA

31 Dixit, A. and R. S. Pindyck (1994) *Investment Under Uncertainty*, Princeton University Press

32 Kahneman, D. Slovic, P. and Tversky A. (1982) *Judgment under Uncertainty: Heuristics and Biases*, Cambridge University Press

33 Shapiro, C. and Varian, H. (1999) *Information Rules: A Strategic Guide to the Network Economy*, Massachusetts: Harvard Business School Press

34 Edler, J. 'Demand-based Innovation Policy', Working Paper No. 9, Manchester Institute of Innovation Research, 2008

35 DTI (2005) *The Empirical Economics of Standards*

36 A frequent cause of failure among firms is an inability to make the transition along the adoption bell-curve and cross the deep and dividing gap – technical, psychological or demographic – that separates early adopters from the mainstream. See Moore, G. (1991) *Crossing the Chasm: Marketing and Selling Technology Products to Mainstream Customers*, HarperCollins

37 Phelps E. (2007) 'The Economic Performance of Nations: Prosperity Depends on Dynamism, Dynamism on Institutions' in Sheshinski, Strom and Baumol eds. *Entrepreneurship, Innovation and the Growth Mechanism of the Free Enterprise Economies*, Princeton University Press

38 Rodrik D. *One Economics, Many Recipes*, Princeton University Press

39 Stern N. (2006) *Stern Review on the Economics of Climate Change*, HM Treasury

40 DCMS (2008) *Creative Economy White Paper*

41 DIUS (forthcoming) *UK 2007 Innovation Survey*

42 European Commission (2005) *Special Eurobarometer "Population Innovation Readiness.*

43 HMT (2006) *The Leitch Review of Skills*

44 Defra (2007) Report of the Commission on Environmental Markets and Economic Performance

45 The Annual Innovation Report will in future incorporate the annual report on the Science and Innovation Investment Framework

46 Baumol W. (2007) 'Sources and Mechanism of Growth' in Sheshinski, Strom and Baumol eds. *Entrepreneurship, Innovation and the Growth Mechanism of the Free Enterprise Economies*, Princeton University Press

47 OGC (2007) *Transforming Government Procurement*

48 OGC (2007) *Finding and Procuring Innovative Solutions*

49 Defra (2007) Report of the Commission on Environmental Markets and Economic Performance

50 DIUS (2008) *Background analysis: strengths and weaknesses of the UK innovation system*

51 DTI (2005) *R&D Intensive Businesses in the UK*

52 DIUS (forthcoming) *UK 2007 Innovation Survey*

53 DIUS (forthcoming) *UK 2007 Innovation Survey*

54 The creative industries include advertising, architecture, the art and antiques market, crafts, design, designer fashion, film, interactive leisure software, music, the performing arts, publishing, software and computer services, television and radio

55 BERR (2008) *Enterprise: Unlocking the UK's Talent*

56 It has grown from 0.04% of GDP in 1997 to 0.08% of GDP in 2004; the US – regarded as the world leader in VC – invested 0.15% of its GDP in both years. In 2006 UK funds managed 57% of Europe's VC and private equity investments, and 33% of European investment from these funds was in the UK – European Private Equity and Venture Capital Association (2007) *EVCA Yearbook*

57 Engineering and Technology Board (2006) *SET and the City: Financing Wealth Creation from Science, Technology and Engineering*

58 Lord Sainsbury of Turville (2007) *The Race to the Top- A Review of Government's Science and Innovation Policies*

59 HM Treasury (2006) *Gowers Review of Intellectual Property*

60 DTI (2005) *The Empirical Economics of Standards*

61 Databuild Research and Solutions (2005) *National Measurement System Impact Assessment.*

62 DTI (2007) *Creativity, design and business performance*

63 Lord Sainsbury of Turville (2007) *The Race to the Top: A Review of Government's Science and Innovation Policies*

# Footnotes

[64] HM Treasury (2004) *Science and Innovation Investment Framework 2004-2014*

[65] Lord Sainsbury of Turville (2007) *The Race to the Top: A Review of Government's Science and Innovation Policies*

[66] Library House (2007) *Spinning out quality: University spin-out companies in the UK*

[67] HM Treasury (2006) *A review of UK health research funding*

[68] Transparent Approach to Costing (TRAC) – see http://www.jcpsg.ac.uk/guidance/about.htm

[69] HM Treasury (2006), *Science and Innovation Investment Framework 2004-2014: next steps*, p26

[70] Recommendation 4.3, Lord Sainsbury of Turville (2007) *The Race to the Top*, p60

[71] DIUS (2008) *Implementing 'The Race to the Top'*

[72] http://www.bio-chip.co.uk/

[73] http://www.foresight.gov.uk/Previous_Projects/Detection_and_Identification_of_Infectious_Diseases/Index.html

[74] OECD (2005) Database on Immigrants and Expatriates

[75] Evidence Limited for the Office of Science and Innovation (2007), *Patterns of international collaboration for the UK and leading partners*

[76] Leadbeater C. (2008) *The Difference Dividend*

[77] Institute of Directors (2007) *Immigration – the business perspective*

[78] OECD (2007) *Moving up the value chain: staying competitive in the global economy*

[79] www.proinno-europe.eu/

[80] HM Treasury (2005) *Lisbon Strategy for Jobs and Growth UK National Reform Programme*

[81] European Commission (26 November 2007).

[82] Report of the Commission for Africa (2005). *Our Common Interest*

[83] http://ec.europa.eu/enterprise/leadmarket/leadmarket.htm

[84] DTI (2006) *Innovation in the UK: Indicators and Insights*

[85] HM Treasury (2006) *The Leitch Review of Skills*

[86] McKinsey & Company & LSE Centre for Economic Performance (2007) *Management practice & productivity: why they matter*

[87] BERR (2008) *BERR's Role in Raising Productivity: New Evidence*

[88] DIUS (2007) *World Class Skills: Implementing the Leitch Review of Skills in England*

[89] LSDA (2005) *Talking the right language: can further education offer support for business innovation*

[90] BERR (2008) *Enterprise: Unloading the UK's Talent*

[91] DIUS (2007) *World Class Skills: Implementing the Leitch Review of Skills in England*

[92] DIUS (2007) *Community Innovation Survey*

[93] Mulgan G. (2007) *Ready or Not: Taking Innovation in the Public Sector Seriously* p4

[94] NESTA (2007), *In and Out of Sync*; Mulgan G., et al., (2006) *Social Silicon Valleys* London: Young Foundation

[95] Prime Minister's Strategy Unit (2006) *The UK Government's Approach to Public Service Reform*

[96] HMT, BERR, CLG (2007) *Sub-National Review of Economic Development and Regeneration*

Printed in the UK for The Stationery Office Limited
on behalf of the Controller of Her Masjety's Stationary Office
ID5748988 03/07

Printed on Paper containing 75% receycled fibre content minimum.